Tall Travel T

Delhi, Agra, Raj

Karen Jennings

Published by Art and Soul Interiors

Edited by Rhys Jennings

ISBN: 978-0-9920826-6-6 (Print Edition)

For Jodi and Carol,
without whom such trips would not be possible.

Contents

And So It Begins...

A middle-aged couple sit in the Pearson International Airport in Toronto, looking tired but happy. They've missed their connecting flight to Ottawa but are content to sit and wait for the next one, nibbling on wasabi-flavoured rice crackers picked up at Narita Airport in Tokyo many hours earlier. The wife leans against her husband, settling comfortably against him while they wait. "Hon," she says, "You know how I've always said I didn't want to go to India? I've changed my mind…" He looks loving at her, his eyebrows raised slightly in surprise. "OK." He smiles. "Let's go!" As an afterthought he muses, "I wonder if we'll have to take our shoes off as often as we did in Japan?

My wonderful husband, Alan, and I recently fulfilled his life-long dream of travelling to Japan. We had a wonderful time trying to speak to the locals in Japanese, eating noodles and spending some nights in traditional inns sleeping on futons on the floor. The journey home was a long one, giving me many hours to sit and think about where we should go next. I knew we would be returning to Japan at some point, but before we did that I figured we should try something a bit different. Japan is organised, clean and efficient. I felt at home there despite obviously being a *gaijin* (foreigner). I towered over the Japanese men and women, had to keep my tattoos covered whenever possible and caused a stir in restaurants when I said I didn't eat meat, but I was comfortable and happy. It's still a bit of a mystery to me why I suddenly decided that India was where I wanted to go next.

It was somewhere I'd never considered going before. A friend works as a pharmacist in a hospital in Vellore and I always read her letters with my mouth hanging open in horror. She reported waiting three days for a train because the scheduled one didn't turn up. She washes her clothes in cold water in a bucket. During the humid season she drips with sweat day and night. Renewing her visa is a nightmare every single time, with long lines, inefficient methods and frustrating bureaucracy. I often shook my head and wondered why she would choose to live there. When talking to people who visited India for a holiday I heard all the usual tales of upset tummies, extreme poverty, smelly sewers and outrageous numbers of beggars. I'd seen movies and read books about people who went to India to "find themselves", which really put me off going because I've never considered myself to be lost. But as I sat on the plane from Tokyo I wondered how I would feel at the end of my life if I'd never been to India. Never eaten a curry in its homeland. Never braved the crowded streets of Delhi. Never tripped in an open sewer and lived to tell the tale. And now, I'm pleased to announce, I've done all of these things and more. India was a wild, exciting, dirty, frustrating adventure, and I'm glad I went. But would I willingly go back? Let me think about that for a while...

The Best Laid Plans...

I decided that the best way for Alan and I to see India would be under the guidance of a small adventure travel company, rather than grabbing our backpacks and travelling alone. It turns out that this was a wise decision and I don't think we would have enjoyed India as much as we did if we had been travelling without our companions and guide. I spent time going through brochures and doing internet searches before placing three options in front of Alan and asking which one he liked the look of. He was still a bit stunned by the fact that I wanted to go to India but he perked up when he realised how much cheaper it would be than returning to Japan. "Is that the cost for both of us?" he asked multiple times. "And this is a *comfort* trip rather than a basic one?" I assured him that he was correct, carefully avoiding mentioning that "comfort" in India was possibly not quite what we would expect to find described as such in Canada. I might have overlooked telling him about the camping in the desert listed on my favourite trip's itinerary, but how bad could that be on a *comfort* tour?

After much deliberation, we settled on a 15-day "Memories of the Maharaja" tour organised by Intrepid Travel, starting in Delhi, moving on to Agra to spend Alan's birthday at the Taj Mahal, then travelling through Rajasthan. Going in November would let us miss the intense heat and humidity of the Indian summer while simultaneously avoiding some of the snowfall in Canada. The tour information sheet promised us a travel specialist, comfortable accommodation, private minibuses for most of the trip, and well-informed local guides. And it was, to a greater or lesser degree, what we got. The highlights of the trip were listed as follows:

- Embark on a camel safari in the desert near Jaisalmer
- See the holy rats of Bikaner's Karni Mata temple
- Experience warm Rajasthani hospitality
- Witness a dramatic sunset over the 'Blue City' of Jodhpur
- Hear the touching story behind the Taj Mahal in Agra
- Stroll through colourful bazaars in Delhi

- Visit the painted havelis of Shekhawati
- Explore the ornate palaces of Jaipur and Udaipur

We did indeed ride camels in the desert, see rats in a temple, spend time in local homes, watch the sun set, visit the Taj Mahal, survive the streets of Delhi, see the crumbling havelis of Shekhawati and follow guides around palaces galore, but nothing was quite like I expected. It was all very *Indian* somehow. But did the folks at Intrepid Travel deliver what they promised? Yes, I have to say they did. They promised us a trip to remember, and remember it we will!

Flights, Medications and Bureaucracy

After deciding which tour to take, I spent time with our travel agent looking at flights to get us from Ottawa in Canada to Delhi in India. Option one, the fastest and most expensive by far, was to fly from Ottawa to Heathrow Airport in London then board a connecting flight to Delhi. This journey would take about 18 hours. A much cheaper option was to fly from Ottawa to Montreal, wait a couple of hours, then get a plane to Frankfurt. After a 7-hour stop over we would get a connecting flight from Frankfurt to Delhi, taking about 30 hours in all. At the time there were no other sensible options on the table so Alan and I opted for the cheaper of the two, reassuring each other that 30 hours "wouldn't be that bad" and we could "grab some sleep in Frankfurt." We thought the journey back would be faster, with the promise of a direct flight from

Frankfurt to Ottawa. As it turned out, Lufthansa cancelled the direct flight and we got to enjoy the delights of Montreal Airport again on the way home. I sometimes wonder if the expensive flights via Heathrow would have been a better choice.

It will come as no surprise to hear that Alan and I are not huge fans of getting sick on holiday, and the thought of getting travellers' diarrhea on a minibus traversing the Indian desert didn't appeal to us. We made an appointment at the travel clinic well before our trip to talk about our medication options and came away with instructions to take DUKORAL®. Not only would this oral vaccine help prevent tummy troubles, but it would also give us some protection against cholera. It was easy to take, although the effervescent drink left me burping more than I considered ladylike. It must have worked because neither of us had upset stomachs in India, unlike during our trip to Jamaica five months later. Next time when something says "Gives protection for 3 months" I'll believe it and take a top-up dose when required!

While at the travel clinic the nurse decided to give us various other boosters and shots. "You should have a course of rabies shots," she enthused, having regaled us with tales of people who went to India and got bitten by random wild animals including dogs and monkeys. "It would ruin your holiday if you got rabies." No kidding! We shuddered at the thought of three separate shots of rabies vaccine, then shuddered again when she told us how much they cost, before conceding to at least discuss it with each other at home. We ultimately decided to have the shots (they go in the arm, not in the abdomen like in the good old days) since they would "hopefully" give us lifetime immunity against the rabies virus. They weren't much fun, and we both felt like utter crap for a while after each shot, but I think it was a good choice to make. We also came away with holes in our arms from tetanus boosters (which came as a complete package including diphtheria and whooping cough vaccines), typhoid inoculations and flu shots "which you might as well have while you're here." Wow. Thanks. We obtained prescriptions for antibiotics to take if the DUKORAL® failed to keep Delhi-belly at bay and left with our arms sore, our pockets full and our wallets empty.

There was some disagreement about the need for malaria pills in Northern India in November, which our nurse thought we should take but I had major reservations about. Drugs don't always agree with me and the risk of side effects from the malaria drugs was quite high. The nurse suggested that I should try Malarone (a combination of atovaquone and proguanil) for four days to see if I had a reaction to the pills before making a final decision about taking them in India. That sounded like a good plan, so I took the prescription to the pharmacy and started drugging myself the next day. The results were quite dramatic and hastened my return to the travel clinic, meeting with the doctor instead of the nurse. "I think it might be better if you don't take them," he said gravely after listening to my long list of side effects after a mere four days of pills. I really didn't want to arrive in India with back and abdominal pain, headaches, nausea, weird dreams, general feelings of irritability and copious amounts of diarrhea. "The risk of getting malaria where you're going is fairly low in November and in your case not taking Malarone would be the best choice. If you happen to catch malaria come see me instead of your family doctor and I'll personally treat you for it." That sounded like a good idea, and I thanked him before running off to the bathroom to engage in something unpleasant. Alan took a course of Malarone pills on holiday with him but stopped taking them after a few days. He said they made him feel "weird".

As it turned out nobody on our tour was bitten by a mosquito, although I was personally nibbled by two small spiders, a large earwig-like insect and numerous sand flies. The day after the tour finished one of our party was bitten on the bottom by a spider and ended up with a large ulcerated lump which had to be lanced by a doctor. Ouch!

In order to enter the potentially bug-laden land of

India, Alan and I needed to obtain tourist visas from the Indian consulate in Ottawa. I went to the website and had a look for application forms, which turned out to be an exercise requiring a lot of time, patience and determination. The Canadian website contained links which shunted me off to a website in India, which in turn told me I had to download the forms from the website in my own country. It allowed me to select "Canada", then returned me to the original website. This, in return, linked back to the Indian website when I tried to access the visa application forms. Talk about being frustrated! When I eventually (and I do mean *eventually*) tracked down the relevant forms, I had to complete them online, then save them. This turned out to be easier said than done, as every time I tried to save my answers the website crashed. This happened again and again. And again. Oh my goodness. Fortunately I'd planned well ahead and could try again on subsequent days until eventually… success! The forms were completed and saved. Phew.

The next step was to print the forms, get them to our local consulate and hand them in. I'm not sure why they couldn't just download them instead of me printing them, but that's the way it was. I looked up the Indian consulate in Ottawa and discovered that they didn't handle visa applications. It had been outsourced to a company called BLS International, which would take the forms and passports to the consulate, collect the visas and then courier them to us. This whole process was estimated to take 7–10 business days, but didn't guarantee that a visa would be granted. "Don't make any travel plans until you have your visa," the website warned. However, in order to apply for the visa you had to complete a section giving details about your trip, including where you would be staying upon arrival in the country. I smiled and shook my head.

An appointment was needed to hand in the visa application forms, so Alan and I selected a date three weeks before our departure, figuring that would allow the necessary 7-10 business days for processing with a bit of slack should something go wrong. We spent 45 minutes in the car and arrived at our appointment on time, application forms in hand. The agent behind the desk glanced at Alan's forms and shook his head without looking up. "You can't apply yet. Come back ten days before you travel." This was news to us. It said nothing about this on any of the websites we'd visited, nor on the appointment booking web site. "How long does it take to get a visa?" I asked. "About seven to ten days," he replied, shuffling some papers on his desk. Alan was starting to look worried, and I shared his concerns. "Can't we just give the forms in now?" I begged. "No. Come back October 26th. You will have to make an appointment." And with that he left, taking his empty coffee cup with him.

Meanwhile, the lady at the next window was having problems of her own. "But I'm Canadian now!" she cried. "You have to bring your landed immigrant document with you," came the reply. "I don't have one. I have a Canadian passport. Why can't I just use that?" Oh dear. We stuffed our forms back into my bag and fled.

We decided to book our second appointment on October 23rd, earlier than the agent suggested, in the hope that we would be able to hand the forms in. We turned up as planned, gave the agent our paperwork and credit cards, paid our fees and left with barely a word spoken. Our passports arrived three days before we were due to leave, with Indian visas securely glued in place, and I'm sure you can imagine how relieved we were!

It's Just Those Bare Necessities

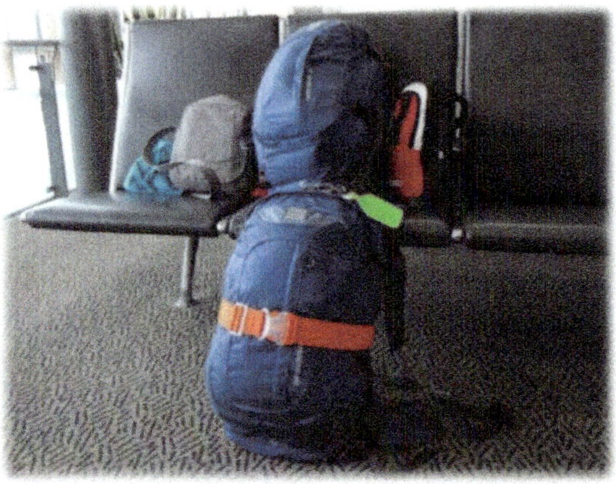

The question of what to take on holiday is an ongoing problem for me. Each time I'm torn between not wanting to take too much stuff and not wanting to arrive without something I really need. As a result, I end up packing more clothes than I actually require and regret lugging around the extra weight. Now don't get me wrong, I'm not the sort of person who packs multiple large suitcases containing 20 dresses, 15 pairs of shoes and a hairdryer for a weekend away, but I always feel like I could have taken less. Packing a backpack for almost three weeks away was my chance to discover how little I really needed and I accepted the challenge gladly. After much deliberation, this is what I settled on.

Footwear: one pair of lightweight fabric walking shoes and one pair of comfortable sandals. *Tops*: five t-shirts in quick-drying fabric, one cardigan and one lightweight long-sleeved top. *Dresses*: one lightweight dress which could be worn as a tunic with leggings. *Bottoms*: one pair of quick-dry multi-pocket long pants, one pair of capris, one pair of leggings and one mid-calf length skirt. *Undies*: not too many, not too few. *Socks*: two pairs. *Headscarves / shawls*: two. *Coats*: one lightweight raincoat, one compact lightweight coat for use in cold airports and Canadian taxis.

I also packed a multitude of medications including the antibiotics prescribed by the travel doctor, antiseptic wipes and cream, eye drops, ear drops, Band-Aids, anti-nausea tablets, painkillers, diarrhea medication and rehydration tablets. I didn't pack any flu medication, figuring that since we'd both had flu shots we wouldn't need it. I also packed two Life Straws and two micro filter refillable water pouches, which would allow Alan and I to drink the water in India without worrying about getting ill from water-borne parasites and bacteria. I stuffed all these things into my backpack along with a few personal items and smiled at the final weight. 15lbs. Alan's pack weighed 18lbs, which he claimed was because his shoes were bigger than mine. We decided not to check our bags for the outward journey, fearing that they might get lost at one of the four airports we would be traversing. We didn't want to arrive in India with the clothes we stood up in, a passport, a visa and very little else!

And They're Off!

The day our adventure began was cold and grey, with snow falling gently from the cloud-covered skies. We tossed our backpacks into a taxi and waved our home, cats and house-sitter a fond farewell. The journey passed fairly uneventfully as we travelled from Ottawa to Montreal then on to Frankfurt, eventually arriving in Indira Ghandi Airport in New Delhi a little weary and disoriented. We'd both tried, and failed, to sleep during the flights, and although Alan had managed to doze off on a bench in Frankfurt Airport neither of us had really slept. Just as a little side note – I have never been as lost and confused in an airport as I was in Frankfurt, despite being able to read and speak some German. It seemed that I had to go through security checks over and over and over again despite never leaving the terminal. Our flight didn't appear on the posted schedules, I couldn't get the "help boards" to work, and it was difficult to find anywhere open to eat. We were due to make a return trip through Frankfurt Airport a few months later on our way home from Amsterdam, and I realised that the 40 minutes allotted to catch our connecting flight simply wouldn't be long enough and would have to be changed. Despite the existence of "fast-track" tunnels there was no way we would make it from one plane to another in time. As it turned out we had to change our flights from Amsterdam completely to add in a stop-over in the UK, but that's a story for another day. "Are you ready?" I asked Alan as we stretched our legs, staggered off the airplane, put on our backpacks and made our way into the customs area in Delhi airport. "Yup," he replied, shaking off the weariness and adjusting his straps. "Let's do India."

We'd arranged to be met at the airport by a representative of Intrepid Travel, but we had no idea where he or she would be waiting. As we exited the customs area we found ourselves surrounded by a vast multitude of people, all holding small signs with names written on them. I looked at Alan in bewilderment. How were we supposed to find our guide in this throbbing, disorganised mess? "You go right and I'll go left," suggested Alan. I set off, looking at sign after sign but seeing nothing relevant. I reached the end of the crowd and returned to meet Alan back in the middle. "Anything?" I asked. "Nope. Perhaps we're supposed to meet him somewhere else?" I looked around, standing on my tiptoes to peer over the mass of people. There *was* nowhere else, and other dazed foreigners were starting to drag their suitcases out of the customs area, adding to the chaos.

"Let's look again. This time you go left and I'll go right," he suggested. I looked at the sea of faces and nodded. "Good luck," I said. I'd nearly reached the end when someone standing about three rows back caught my eye and held his sign higher. My heart leapt. Could this be him? I read his sign and my heart sank again. "Mr and Mrs Conwell" it said. I shook my head sadly and the man lowered his sign, disappearing back into the crowd.

And then I saw it. A man in the crowd was grasping a small sign with about six travel companies written on it, and in the top right hand corner were the tiny words "Peregrine Travel"- the sister company of Intrepid. I saw Alan heading back towards me, looking glum, and I waved him to walk faster. "Do you think it might be him?" I asked, gesturing to the man I'd spotted. "It might be! Let's go and ask." We pushed passed some fellow tourists and stood in front of the Peregrine man. "Are you from Intrepid?" Alan asked. The guy nodded. "We're Alan and Karen Jennings. Are you here to meet us?" He nodded again, and then we all just stood there looking at each other for a while. Eventually I broke the silence. "Are we waiting for anyone else?" He shook his head. "So can we go?" Our guide hesitated before replying. "Have you exchanged money? Got rupees? You must do it here." We assured him that we'd bought rupees before leaving the main terminal and he seemed a bit happier. "OK. We go to taxi. Follow me. Don't go with anyone else. Just me."

We followed him outside, brushing off the men calling "You want taxi? Best price!" "You want me to carry your bag?" "Where you from?" "I take you where you go fast!" As we exited the building the smell greeting us was overwhelming. It wasn't the expected odour of sewers and spices but an exhaust-fume smog so thick that it was hard to breathe. I looked at Alan, who raised his eyebrows. "This wasn't quite what I thought India would smell like," he spluttered. Our guide relieved us of our backpacks, bundled us into a taxi and slammed the door. "Hotel Jivitesh," he told the driver, and off we went.

It was the wee hours of the morning but the roads from the airport to New Delhi were quite busy. They were wide and paved like the ones back home, but that's where the similarity ended. Canadian roads are orderly. Drivers stick (more or less) to clearly defined rules, most of which didn't appear to apply in India. Our taxi weaved through the traffic, the driver keeping one hand on the steering wheel and the other on the horn. All around us were taxi cabs, honking ceaselessly, with pale, tired-looking tourists in the back seats. Tuk-tuks swerved in and out between cars while trucks chugged along wherever they pleased regardless of any lane markings on the road. Alan and I looked at each other and grinned. This was going to be a fun trip.

Our cab dropped us off at the Jivitesh Hotel in New Delhi, leaving after we tipped both him and our guide. The lady at reception took photocopies of our passports and directed us up to our room. In the dim light it looked comfortable and inviting, but I was desperate to wash off some of the travel grime before falling into bed. I turned on the shower and waited for the water to get hot. And waited. And waited. Eventually I realised that there was no hot water at 3am in the Hotel Jivitesh and braved the cold spray. As I rolled into bed next to Alan he enquired "How was it?" "The water pressure was good," I grinned in the darkness.

I slept like the dead, waking around 8am to the sounds of Alan showering. "How's the water?" I yelled. "Cool," came the reply. I laughed and got out of bed. Through the dirt-covered windows I could see traffic weaving around on the dual carriageway outside the hotel, honking merrily. Most of the grime was on the outside of the window, but the bottom two inches on the inside were coated with a thick layer of pink mildew, which must have been accumulating for months. The rest of the room was pretty, clean and well maintained, so I pulled down the blind to hide the mildew and decided to pretend it wasn't there.

Once we were both clean and dressed, Alan and I wandered down to the small dining room for breakfast. A vegetarian buffet was laid out with treats such as pickles, vegetable croquettes and lentil soup. A waiter appeared at my side as I tried to decide what to sample first. "Would you like a dosa?" he asked. Oh my word! I *love* dosa, especially since I find the thin fermented pancakes almost impossible to make myself. I chose the masala dosa while Alan chose the plain one, and they both arrived hot, crispy and paper-thin a few minutes later. This was a fabulous start to the day, especially when eaten with sambhar (lentils) and coconut chutney.

We'd arrived in India a day prior to our tour starting and we wanted to make the most of the opportunity to see the sights of Delhi. The easiest, if not the cheapest, way to do this was to hire a taxi and driver for the day, which could be arranged at the front desk in the hotel. We spoke to the concierge, agreed on a price and was told our driver would be waiting for us outside in 10 minutes. He then gave each of us the hotel's business card along with the warning to keep it with us "in case of any problems." This was repeated at every place we stayed in India, along with the instructions to keep the hotel's business cards with us at all time "in case we got lost." We went back to our room, grabbed our cameras and water bottles and prepared ourselves to have some fun.

Delhi

Our taxi driver was waiting for us as promised in the hotel courtyard. I was happy to see that while his car had various scratches it had no visible major collision damage, giving me some confidence in his ability to traverse the roads of Delhi safely. "Where would you like to go today?" he asked. Alan got out his map and pointed out places we *didn't* want to go as we would be seeing them on our tour. "So I take you to Indian Parliament first? Show you good building? Then we go here," he pointed at the map, "here, here and maybe here..." Ajay had obviously done tours such as this before, so we were happy to agree with his suggestions. We pulled out of the courtyard and into the honking traffic, which not surprisingly was even crazier on a Saturday morning than it had been at 3am. Vehicles packed the road. Lane markings were taken as mere suggestions and weaving between them while honking loudly was totally acceptable.

Motorcycles swerved in and out of small gaps, often with entire families on board. Sari-clad women sat sideways on the back of the motorcycles holding babies and men drove with toddlers on their laps. Some people wore helmets, most did not, as they participated in the traffic-dance. Roundabouts were circumnavigated in both directions, traffic lights were regarded as warnings rather than something to be obeyed, and pedestrians were an annoyance to be driven around. It was all quite, quite mad, but somehow the traffic kept moving and we slowly headed towards our first sight-seeing destination.

India's Parliament Buildings and the India Gate

Ajay's tour started with a visit to the parliament building, which he told us is one of the most impressive structures in India. I had to take his word for it as it was hard to see anything through the haze of smog filling the air. "Can you stop the car so we can take a closer look?" I asked. "I can't stop here. But perhaps if I stop over there and you walk quickly, take a few photos and come back fast we will be OK."

I looked at the armed guards standing around and decided to risk it. Alan grabbed his camera, I grabbed mine and we quickly took a few shots before leaping back into the car. Ajay shot off at some speed, obviously wanting to get away before he got into trouble. "A lot of the buildings here were designed by the British," he told us as he sped along the deserted street. "But we leave here now and go to the India Gate. I park, and you go look for as long as you want."

India Gate was originally called the All India War Memorial, and is only a few minutes' drive down wide, tree-lined roads from Parliament Street. Ajay parked and as soon as we got out Alan and I were surrounded by people selling souvenirs and useless junk. "You want a wood flute? I play it for you. Good sound!" "You want postcard? Look - many pictures!" "Buy whistle from me! Best whistle here! Good price for tourist!" We pushed our way through as politely as we could and headed towards the gate. The area was very busy. Foreign tourists jockeyed to take photos of each other underneath the gate while fighting off hawkers. "You want candy floss? I make it myself! Good price for two bags!" Local families sat on the grass eating picnics while their children played tag or kicked soccer balls around.

Alan and I fought our way to the gate and paused to read some of the names inscribed in the stone. An eternal flame burned underneath the arch, solemnly guarded by a soldier amidst the hordes of sightseers. Taking decent photographs was impossible under the circumstances but we were lucky enough to make a return trip to the gate after our Rajasthan tour ended, allowing us to photograph it on a clear, smogless day unencumbered by hundreds of other tourists.

Before returning to our taxi we paused to look at an empty stone canopy, inspired by a 6th century pavilion. It used to cover a 50ft tall marble statue of King George V, but the statue itself was relocated in the 1960's. There has been talk over the years of replacing the missing statue with one of Mahatma Ghandi, but nothing has happened yet.

Humayun's Tomb Complex

Our next stop was at the world heritage site Humayun's tomb, the construction of which began in 1565 under the watchful eyes of Hamida Banum Begum, 9 years after the death of her husband, the Mughal Emperor Humayun. The Persian-style palace-like structure was finished in 1572, inspired by the tomb of Humayun's ancestor Tamerlane in Uzbekistan. It was the first tomb of its kind to be built in India, placed in the middle of a garden divided into four sections to resemble the paradise garden written about in the Quran. It, in turn, was the inspiration behind the Taj Mahal, which was built to house the remains of Humayun's grandson's wife many years later.

The tomb was much more impressive than I'd anticipated, sitting on a raised platform with an arched terrace surrounding the dome-topped central building. Inside was an octagonal room containing the graves of various members of the royal family, but I'm not sure who was buried where, as signs were few and far between. I don't think I saw the grave of the emperor himself, which I believe lies somewhere in the basement.

There are various other tombs in the grounds surrounding Humayun's final resting place, including that of Isa Khan Niyazi, who was a noble in the Sher Shah Sur court. The octagonal structure was crammed full of seemingly randomly designed graves, housing, I assume, the remains of Isa's relatives alongside Isa himself. Despite the heat and humidity of the day it was cold and damp inside the tomb, so I didn't linger to find out who was buried where and left them in peace.

Lunch with the Locals

By now Alan and I were quite hot, tired, possibly a bit tetchy and feeling the effects of a ten and a half-hour time change, so we asked Ajay if he could take us somewhere for lunch. "Cheap or expensive?" he enquired. "Cheap," I replied. "Expensive," Alan countered. "We don't want to get an upset stomach on our first day." "Perhaps somewhere not too cheap but not really expensive?" I suggested. Ajay nodded, pulled into the stream of traffic while honking his horn enthusiastically, and off we went. We hadn't gone very far when he abruptly pulled over near the side of the road. "Get out here. Go through the gap in the wall. When you finish walk along the road and I find you." I looked blankly at Alan, who shrugged in reply. "Quick. Quick. I don't stop here. Get out now," Ajay insisted.

With some reservation Alan and I disembarked and watched our taxi drive away. We knew he would come back at some point since we hadn't paid him yet, but we had no idea where we were or what type of restaurant he'd brought us to. Alan took my hand and led me towards the gap in the wall. Other than some pictures of deities painted on the wall underneath the word "welcome" there was no indication that a restaurant lay within.

We walked along a winding pathway lined with lush green plants and emerged into a courtyard filled with dining tables, cabanas and tree stumps topped with cushions. A buffet was laid out under the canopy of large trees and at the end of the courtyard was a long table displaying various dishes in heated pots. But the thing which struck me most about this lunch spot was the people. We were the only white faces to be seen, and the only people dressed in "travel clothes". You know what I mean - comfy sandals, multi-pocketed pants, quick-dry t-shirts. The best I can say about my personal attire is that it didn't have any stains on it and I'd topped it off with a flowing hand-painted scarf. The other female diners wore beautiful embroidered saris or pristine European-style dresses with fabulous footwear. "Oh my goodness," I whispered to Alan. "They're all wearing Louboutin shoes!" He looked at me blankly. "They're, like, $800 a pair!" His eyebrows shot up, but I'm not sure if that's because he was astounded by the cost of red-soled shoes or because he didn't expect me to know the price of designer footwear. The men were dressed in shirts and ties, with hand-stitched jackets thrown casually over the backs of their chairs. "I'm thinking this place isn't going to be cheap," I murmured in Alan's ear.

A waiter wearing white gloves appeared as if by magic. "Please take a seat," he said, gesturing to a white-linen covered table for two. He produced menus with a flourish.

"Everything you see here (he waved his arms expansively) is included in the buffet price. If you want alcoholic drinks there is an extra charge." I took a quick look at the menu, immediately heading for the drinks section. "I'll have a Kingfisher please," I said. Alan nodded. "I'll have one too." I'd seen the price of the buffet on the back of the menu, and I thought a drink or two might be needed to soften the blow.

I've never paid as much for lunch as I did in that Indian garden restaurant. I wish I could add that it was the best lunch I've ever had, but I'd be lying. Alan faired OK, sampling roast meats, chicken dishes, chocolate-laden freshly cooked waffles and ice-cream, but for me the selection was severely limited. I don't eat meat, fish, seafood, eggs or dairy. Yes, you've got it. I'm vegan. But honestly, I'm quite nice when you get to know me. I settled for a bowl of steamed rice topped with veggies fried in olive oil, followed by some sliced melon. It was OK, but definitely not worth what it cost. As we paid the bill Alan and I agreed that next time a taxi driver asked us if we wanted a cheap lunch or an expensive one we would say "cheap." Preferably *very* cheap!

We exited the courtyard through the wall and looked around for any sign of Ajay. The road was lined with luxury vehicles, but our taxi was nowhere to be seen. "Let's walk down the road and see if he's parked somewhere," I suggested. We'd not gone very far when we heard someone honking vigorously behind us. It was Ajay, who pulled over just long enough for us to leap in before moving away as I pulled the door closed. "Did you enjoy lunch?" he asked. I caught Alan's eye. "It was... interesting," I replied. "There were lots of different food and some very expensive shoes." "Yes," he said, "it's where the rich people of Delhi go for brunch. I hope you enjoyed it?" I assured him that we had, although I might not have been completely truthful. I didn't want to hurt his feelings. "But next time a cheap Indian restaurant perhaps?" he added with a grin.

Qutb Minar

Our next destination was the Qutb Minar, also known as the Qutub or Qutab Minar. Construction of this tower and the temple nearby started in 1193, but there seems to be some debate about why it was built. Some say it was simply a minaret erected to call Muslims to prayer while others say it was built to commemorate the demolition of 27 Hindu temples and the beginning of Muslim rule of India. The basement was built during the reign of Qutab-ud-din Aibak, the first Muslim ruler of Delhi, with three stories added by his successor, Iltutmush. The top story was added by Firoz Shah Tughlak in 1368.

It was as we paid to enter this heritage site that I began to appreciate something I had been hearing over and over again since we arrived in Delhi. "Special price for tourists!" We'd been warned before travelling that salespeople in India would take advantage of us as foreigners and extract as much money from us as they possibly could. But it wasn't until I read the entrance fees at the minar that I truly understood the situation. The fee for Indian people was 10 rupees but they charged foreigners 250 rupees – twenty-five times the local rate! I was speechless. I had expected to pay more... maybe double the price... but nothing like this. We were being gouged, and everyone knew it. Throughout our trip we were overcharged by anyone and everyone, everywhere. Yes, we haggled whenever possible but we still walked away paying much more than we should have. "Special price for tourists!" No kidding!

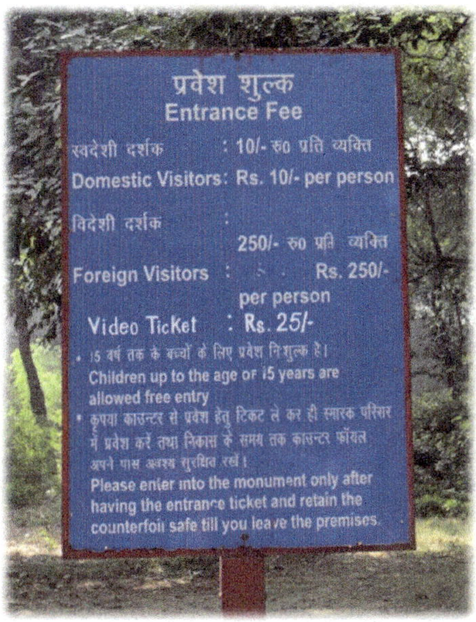

Walking into the Minar complex, I stopped to admire the beautiful carvings on a pillar while local tourists streamed by. Then something strange happened. As I stood there taking pictures I became aware of an ever-increasing group of Indian men also taking pictures. I stepped back to give them a better view, and they all stepped back too. I shot Alan a querying look. "They're trying to take photos of each other with you,"

he said. I looked at the closest man, and he looked away guiltily. "What are you doing?" I asked another guy as he manoeuvred behind me and gestured to his friend to take a photo. He shrugged and gave his friend a thumbs up. "Go away," I told a third as I headed back to Alan. "What the hell are they doing?" I asked him. "I think it's your arm," he said, nodding towards my tattoo. Ah. That might explain it.

As we turned to walk away a group of young men surrounded us while another took up a position with his camera poised. "Ali Baba!" he yelled at Alan as his friends posed for a picture with us. Oh dear. I could hide my tattoo if necessary, but there wasn't a lot we could do about Alan's red beard. During our time in India we had to endure being photographed almost everywhere we went whether we wanted it or not and, to be honest, it was a total pain in the ass. I won't mention it over and over again throughout the book, but please assume that at almost every attraction I visit, and almost every time I stand still or sit down, there is someone nearby having a photo taken with me. It's never a woman, it's always a loud, rude, inconsiderate, usually young, male. Or two. Or three. Ugh.

The Qtub Minar complex was filled with people milling around or lounging on the crumbled stones of the once beautiful temple. The tower itself was still standing, but every other building was in ruins. Every now and again we came across a wall which was mostly intact, standing alone in the middle of piles of rubble. They must have been fabulous when they were first built, and it was sad to see how the mighty had fallen.

Safdarjang's Tomb

The next stop on what was rapidly turning into a *tombs of Delhi* tour was the mausoleum built in 1754 in memory of Safdarjang (Mirza Abul Masur Khan), who was the prime minster of the Mughal Empire in 1748. It was the last of the garden tombs to be built and bears a striking resemblance to both Humayun's tomb and the Taj Mahal. The red sandstone and marble used to make it were taken from the tomb of Abdur Rahim Khan-i-Khana, and according to the information board at the site the tomb is "the last flicker in the dying lamp of Mughal architecture in Delhi". On the day of our visit the lamp appeared to have died completely. We pulled into a deserted parking lot and looked for the ticket office. We found it set into in the crumbling outer walls of the complex and paid for our (special price for tourists) tickets under the watchful eyes of a girl piling up pebbles at the other end of the row of arches.

In contrast to the other places we had already visited, this tomb was almost completely deserted. We encountered two or three other couples before we left the mausoleum, but the place really was as quiet as a grave. There was no water in the pond, no fountains spraying jets into the air, no children running around laughing, and no young men trying to take photos of weird foreigners. It was all quite sad, really.

Swaminarayan Akshardham

"Where to next?" Ajay asked us as we sank back into the taxi feeling somewhat deflated after out visit to Safdarjang's tomb. "I don't know," Alan sighed. "Where do you recommend?" "We go to Swaminarayan Akshardham," he declared after a moment of thought. "It will be busy, but you will like it."

As we drove off we passed a naked man strolling along at the side of the road, followed by a small crowd of people wearing saffron-coloured robes. "Is that normal in India?" I asked Ajay. He shrugged in reply. "Not as much as it used to be. He's a naked Sadhu, probably heading to a temple. The people behind him have taken him as their guru." He presented this information with disinterest, reminding me how different attitudes are between Canada and India. A naked man on the streets of Ottawa would quickly find himself in trouble. In Delhi he was just one more naked man on his way to the temple.

It wasn't long before Ajay pulled the car over on a wide bridge and suggested we get out to photograph a temple on the horizon. "That's where we're going, but you can't take any photos when you are there. This is as close as you can get with your camera." We stood on the bridge and took some unimpressive zoomed-in shots which even Photoshop struggled to make look decent. We were quite a distance from the temple, and the air was thick with smog, but we could see that the complex covered quite a large area.

We pulled into a huge, packed parking lot near the temple and Ajay told us to remember where he was parked. "Many, many cars," he warned us. "Don't forget where you must come back to." We took note of our location and headed off across the immense lot towards the entrance. Alan stood in the men's line and I joined the women waiting to pass through the security gates and metal detectors before walking through the "welcome gates" to the beautifully carved stone entrance known as the Bhakti Dwar (Gate of Devotion). After the ruins we had seen at today's tombs it took my breath away to see such splendor – and this was merely the entrance!

Once inside the opulent visitors' center we were greeted by a young lady in beautifully embroidered clothing. "Please do not take any photographs in or around our complex," she said in perfect, accentless English. "This is a sacred place and we wish everyone to enjoy it in peace and harmony." I promised to leave my camera in my bag but expressed sadness that I wouldn't be able to show my friends how beautiful it was when we returned home. "Don't worry," she said. "You can buy our guide, which has lots of beautiful pictures." So I did, and she was correct. It really does contain some beautiful pictures, but I can't share them with you. I'll do my best to describe some of the things we saw, but to truly appreciate the awesome carvings you will have to go there yourself.

Outside the visitors' center was a huge courtyard containing a small square red marble pool surrounded by people. I wandered over to get a closer look. At each corner a golden conch shell squirted water into the pool, splashing onto two large white marble feet covered in symbols. I raised my eyebrows at Alan and he shrugged. "I have no idea," he said in answer to my unvoiced question. Fortunately there was a sign by the pool explaining that it contained a replica of the holy footprints of Bhagwan Swaminarayan, who died in 1830. I have to admit that I didn't really feel much wiser after learning this, but it was interesting nonetheless.

Walking away from the feet towards the main central building - the Akshardham Mandir - I paused to leave our shoes at the designated drop-off stall. This was the first of many occasions I would find myself barefoot in India and it was by far the cleanest and best organised shoe-depository I would encounter.

The spotlessly clean Akshardham Mandir opened in 2005. Around 11,000 artisans and volunteers built the complex in under 5 years, which was an incredible achievement. The mandir itself was built as a home for God and displays the principals of traditional Hindu Indian architecture. There are 20 four-sided spires, 234 pillars, 9 domes and 20,000 statues of

Indian Hindu personalities. Each pillar inside the mandir is covered with intricate carvings of deities or tells a story from the life of Bhagwan Swaminarayan. Carvings also cover the walls and ceilings. It was truly breathtaking. The central shrine of the mandir houses a huge golden statue of Bhagwan Swaminarayan. Born in 1781, he was a hugely influential figure in the social reforms which happened in India. He forbade violent sacrifices, stopped female infanticide and allowed women to get an education. He preached a faith based on the four pillars of "bhakti, dharma, spirituality and a detachment from worldly ignorance" and is believed by his followers to have been the human manifestation of "the Supreme God". The statue of Swaminarayan is joined in the shrine by several other "divine gurus" to whom devotees pray.

We left the beauty inside the temple and set off on our barefoot walk around the outside under the watchful eyes of security guards. Periodic shouts of "You can't sit there," and "Don't touch that," broke the tranquility as tourists demonstrated themselves to be less than perfect worshippers. Carvings of elephants and lions covered the lower part of the temple walls, above which was a carved layer of flowers and plants. Statues stood in ornate alcoves framed by decorated columns. If you find yourself in Delhi this really is somewhere you should visit.

There were other activities taking place within the complex which we chose not to purchase tickets for. Had we had either the time or the inclination we could have visited the "hall of values", watched an epic movie about a young man travelling across the Indian subcontinent, or taken a short "cultural boat ride" back through time.

By now Alan and I were both quite tired, and the day was nearing an end. We somehow managed to find Ajay and his chariot and asked that he take us back to our hotel. "Sure," he said. "But first I take you to a very good shop owned by my friend. It is a family store. Lots of things to buy and very good price for tourists." I couldn't help laughing. When we made a purchase the store owner took cash from the till and gave our driver his cut of the profits.

Dinner for Two

When Ajay dropped us back at the hotel after the obligatory tour of his friend's shop we gave him a tip and asked him if he knew anywhere nearby for a cheap dinner, specifying that we wanted a curry. "Yes," he said, "my friend has a restaurant near here. Leave the hotel and go left. Keep walking and you will get to it. Very good food." We thanked him and went to our room to shower off the sweat and grime of the day's adventures, happy to discover that hot water was available. Feeling refreshed, we asked at the front desk for a second opinion on somewhere to eat close by. "It doesn't matter which way you go," she replied. "There are many places to eat. But walk carefully and don't fall in the holes. Don't get into a tuk-tuk outside. Plenty of places to walk to." We thanked her and headed out the door. We'd gone about three steps when the tuk-tuk drivers accosted us. "You want dinner? I take you to my friend's restaurant. Very good food. You like! Very good price to take you there, and I wait to bring you back!" We shook our heads and kept walking. "You no walk!" came cries of horror behind us "Is not safe! I drive you. Very fast. Good food!" We turned right and kept going, being careful not to trip or fall off the sidewalk (I use the term loosely) into the honking traffic.

We'd walked for maybe five minutes before spotting a small restaurant up some steps. It had locals sitting at the tables, and it looked clean and inviting. And the smell wafting in the air was fabulous even tainted with the odour of the ever-present smog. We went in and were shown to a table by a surprised-looking waiter. "You want to eat here?" he asked. We assured him that we did indeed wish to eat, and he brought us a menu. There were lots of vegetarian options to choose from and, after checking that they didn't contain dairy, I made my selection. The dishes arrived piping hot, served with naan bread and basmati rice. We'd had a busy day and wolfed down every last bite. It was delicious.

Apparently I was also delicious. I left the restaurant with two red itchy bites, courtesy of a small spider I saw jumping off my arm and hurrying away.

Being Taken For a Ride

Our tour was due to start after lunch the next day, leaving us with a free morning to further explore the delights of Delhi. Determined to make the most of every minute, we got an early start with breakfast (those dosa were just *so* good!) and decided to get a tuk-tuk from outside the hotel to do a bit more touring. Alan and I had both read a book called "Delirious Delhi" by Dave Prager in which he wrote about his frequent trips to Connaught Place. This shopping district is made up of a central hub surrounded by three concentric circles of streets and is claimed to be Delhi's number one district for both shopping and entertainment. On the map it didn't seem to be far from where we were staying, so it was the obvious place to go when we had a free morning.

We told the guy at the hotel travel-assistance desk what we were planning to do and he assured us that Connaught Place would be worth a visit. We later realised there was something that he should have mentioned on this smoggy Sunday morning, but perhaps it slipped his mind. He asked if we wanted to hire a taxi, warning us that the tuk-tuk drivers outside would overcharge us. We decided to throw caution to the wind and risk financial ruin by going in a tuk-tuk, not wanting to miss out on experience of travelling along the busy roads in such a vehicle. We saw tuk-tuks everywhere - each one painted green with a yellow roof, every one of them scratched or dented, all chugging along with just enough power to not require a push up slight hills. And all honking... honking... honking as they swerved in and out of traffic. It looked like fun.

We grabbed our day packs and stepped out of the hotel into the fume-laden air. We'd only taken a few steps when a tuk-tuk driver hurried over, eager to catch his prey. "You want tuk-tuk? I take you to shops? Good price!" We glanced back at the hotel doorman to see if he was worried about us travelling with this man. He caught my eye and shrugged, which I took as meaning "He's OK. Go ahead." Although, of course, it could also have meant "You're stupid foreign tourists who don't know anything. Do whatever you want." We told the driver that we wanted to go to Connaught Place to do some shopping and he happily agreed to take us there, wait for us and then bring us back when we had finished. "Is it a good place to go?" Alan asked. "Oh yes. Very nice. Lots of shops and places to eat. Very good place. I take you." And once again, someone neglected to mention something which later turned out to be important.

We haggled a price, knowing we were being

overcharged despite the negotiating, and prepared to get into his waiting tuk-tuk. "No, no." He waved his hands at us. "This is not mine. You wait here one minute." And with that he turned and left. Alan and I looked at each other in bewilderment. Was this guy a tuk-tuk driver or not? We looked around at the other drivers, hoping for some sort of sign, but they ignored us. A tuk-tuk pottered towards us from a side street and our driver waved for us to get in. "Connaught Place please," said Alan. "Yes, yes," came the reply. "Very nice place." And off we went.

According to the map, our destination wasn't far away. Google maps said 13 minutes by car, 40 minutes on foot. After a while Alan and I began to suspect that either our driver didn't know where Connaught Place was, or that he wasn't actually taking us there directly. "Where are you going?" Alan asked. "I take you shopping like you asked," came the rather vague reply. "Are you taking us to Connaught Place?" "Yes, yes, very nice place. Good for shopping. What you want to buy?" I tapped Alan's knee and pointed at a bike leaning against a closed storefront. "This is the second time we've driven past this," I whispered. "We're going round in circles."

Our driver must have heard me because he loudly declared "Nearly there! Not far now!" Our thirteen-minute drive had so far taken us twenty-five minutes or so, and we had no idea where we were. A few minutes later he turned up an alley and parked outside the only open store on the dirty street. "You go in here. Good shop. You find everything here. Clothes, statues, rugs. Anything you want. Go in! Go in!" This was *not* Connaught Place. This was a dirty, dingy little shop up some back alley, owned by someone who would give him money for taking tourists there. "No," said Alan. "This is not where we want to go. Take us to Connaught Place." Our driver folded his arms and settled in his seat. "You go in here first. Everything you need. Good prices for tourists." I gestured to Alan and we got out, then started walking away down the alley. Our driver leapt out of the tuk-tuk and called after us anxiously "Where you going? Go in this shop!" "No," I replied. "We're going to find someone who will take us to Connaught Place. We're not paying you. This isn't where we want to go." Our driver was quite distraught. "You can't walk here! Not safe! Not safe! Get back in and I take you where you want to go. But first, look inside here!" I groaned.

"Let's just have a quick look to keep him happy," suggested Alan, so we turned round and entered the store. We were immediately surrounded by assistants asking us what we wanted to see and assuring us that they had the very best prices. Maybe they did, and maybe they didn't, but we had no intension of buying anything which we would have to lug around India for the next two weeks. We thanked them for showing us their goods, said it all looked very nice then left. "What you buy?" enquired our driver. "Nothing. Now take us to Connaught Place." He sighed and started the engine. Five minutes later we were driving around the empty streets of Connaught Place looking at the boarded-up store fronts. What was the important thing nobody had thought to mention to us? Connaught Place is closed on Sunday mornings.

Old Delhi

We grabbed lunch in the hotel restaurant and looked at the people sitting at other tables, suspecting that they would be our fellow travellers for the next 15 days. When we congregated in the lounge shortly afterwards we discovered we were right. We sat waiting for our tour guide to arrive, all looking a little uncomfortable and not speaking. After what seemed to be an eternity, a young man entered the room. "Namaste," he said, then introduced himself in perfect English. He was to be our guide for the tour and had been working for Intrepid / Peregrine Tours for quite a while. We were definitely not his first group of worried tourists, and he promised to try not to lose any of us. "My name is Purushottam but it's very hard for people to pronounce," he said, "so you can call me 'Puru'. Introduce yourselves to the group," he suggested. And so we did.

Grace and Ada, hereafter referred to as "The Aunties" were retired, well-travelled sisters from New Zealand. I had a lot of trouble telling them apart but I know they were both fun to be around and, despite being the oldest in the group, they were sometimes hard to keep up with. Also from New Zealand was Shannon, an educational specialist for children with special needs. Lily, an air hostess, did a fabulous job of representing England by being beautiful, bubbly and the centre of attention wherever we went. Ryan, who joined us the following day, originated in Northern Ireland and was travelling for some fun before settling down in Australia. Alan and I were the only Canadians in the group; the remainder were all from Australia. Linus and Lucinda were a middle-aged couple from Sydney making a return visit to India after backpacking through the country in their younger days. Janice and Jasmina were a mother-daughter team travelling together before Janice set off on further adventures in Peru, Bolivia and Argentina. Angie was a police officer and Loretta worked for the Taronga Conservation Society. Last, but by no means least, was Beth, a psychologist from Sydney. Our ages ranged from early 20's to late 70's but despite the generation gaps we all got along famously. You won't ever meet a nicer group of people, and it was a real pleasure to experience India with this motley crew. They'll pop up in the story from time to time, and I hope you enjoy their company as much as I did. I've changed everyone's names in the book, including our guide and various drivers, not because I've forgotten them but to preserve their privacy.

The travel guide for the "Memories of the Maharaja Tour" promised us that we would "dive straight in to the chaos of Delhi, India's pulsating capital" and, true to form, Puru ushered us out into the street as soon as the introductions were over. We were taking a ride on the Metro into Old Delhi. It wasn't a long walk to the closest train station but it was fraught with danger as we slipped into potholes and the dodged traffic weaving haphazardly along the busy road. Before entering the station itself Puru suggested we buy water from a stall selling bottles. The day was a hot one, and we were already all looking in need of a drink after only a short walk. After replenishing our supply of liquids, we climbed the steps into the train station where Puru bought tickets for us all. Armed guards stood around, waving threateningly at anyone holding a camera. "No pictures!"

We followed Puru through security checks and onto the platform where he directed the ladies to the "women only" area. It was considered unwise for foreign women to join the men in the mixed carriages as there was a strong risk of undesirable contact from overly friendly local males. "Don't forget to get off to change trains!" Puru warned. We nodded and huddled together, fearing being separated from each other this early in our trip. Puru led Alan and Linus away and were soon lost from view in the ever-growing crowd.

We got to know each other quite intimately on the two trains we took into Old Delhi, packed into the carriage with a multitude of sari-clad women. I towered over the local ladies, whose heads bounced into my bosom every time the train jerked. I was quite grateful not to be in the mixed sex carriage. We successfully changed trains and all arrived at the Old Delhi station no worse for wear, although it was quite a relief to regain an inch or two of personal space. I should have enjoyed this more while it lasted - personal space was a luxury which didn't exist on the streets of Old Delhi.

Puru did a head-count and beckoned for us to follow him. "If you get lost, use your hotel business cards and take a taxi back to the hotel," he warned. "Don't take a tuk-tuk. Don't try to get a train. Take a taxi. But it would be better if you didn't get lost!" And with that he led us out of the station and into the hot, crowded, fragrant streets of Delhi. The pathway leading from the station was lined with stalls selling western-style clothing, saris and jewellery. Food vendors were cooking thin pancakes stuffed with vegetables or serving up plates of freshly sliced fruit. Puru paused to show us some miniature wooden houses nailed to a tree, explaining that it was important to be kind to insects in case we came back as one in our next life.

We emerged onto a main street which Puru crossed with barely a pause. I looked at Alan and he took my hand. "Just walk." We stepped into the traffic, which swerved round us as if we were part of a dance as we kept moving forwards regardless of what was heading towards us. I gave him a grin as we arrived safely at the other side, then turned to watch the others cross. The Aunties were doing what I can only describe as a chicken dance, stepping forwards then backwards, stopping and starting, squealing as they went. I couldn't help but laugh. When they eventually arrived I gave them a bit of advice. "Just walk forwards, don't jump backwards. The drivers are expecting you to go in one direction, and you're much more likely to get hit if you take a step back." They nodded and agreed to try it. At the next road we had to cross they managed it like professionals, looking drivers in the eye and marching forwards relentlessly. They totally aced it.

As I peered over heads at the buildings of Old Delhi I

realised it was aptly named. Everything looked very old indeed, somewhat dilapidated and covered in grime. It was a mishmash of buildings built on top of each other, all badly in need of repairs and a paint job. But on a Sunday afternoon it was extremely busy, crammed wall to wall with shoppers, all jostling to make their way through the streets.

Chandni Chowk

Puru was taking us to the Chandni Chowk, the old marketplace of Delhi. It was absolute chaos with cars, motorcycles, tuk-tuks, rickshaws and the occasional cow competing with pedestrians for space to manoeuvre. Puru gathered his flock together and pointed to one of the small alleys. "We're going this way. Stay together, don't get lost and protect your valuables. Don't have anything in your pockets." And with that he pushed his way into the crowd, his baseball cap barely visible in the mass of people. We followed him, shuffling along slowly, making bodily contact with people at every step. I'd assumed the alleyways would be for pedestrians only, but I couldn't have been more wrong. People on motorcycles slowly eased their way through the crowds. Men pulling heavily laden carts shoved their way through, slowly making their way to their intended store. Tuk-tuks honked relentlessly as pedestrians blocked their way. It was utter chaos. Overhead the air was filled with cables, intertwined to form a mad spider's web.

I can't imagine anyone actually going to this market to do some shopping and actually being successful as the mass of people and traffic made it almost impossible to see the store fronts, much less make it through the door and into a shop. But for those who wanted to buy something, I'm sure there was a shop selling whatever they needed. Over the heads of the throng of people I spotted coin sellers, sari shops, food vendors, jewellery stores, kitchen wares, electronic stores and shoe shops. Street food was being cooked on small stalls jammed into corners, and the smells wafting through the air were amazing. As I pushed my way along I made sure I could always see at least one other member of Puru's flock, even though the man himself was usually hidden from sight. He stopped periodically to do a headcount and was obviously enjoying his trip through the market. I suspect he was laughing at the dazed looks on our faces as we all battled our way through, standing on toes, shoulder-checking little old ladies and trying to move out of the way of determined rickshaw drivers. After a while he stopped on a corner and waited patiently until we had all arrived, grabbing the arm of the less observant ones as they wandered by without noticing him. It was time for tea.

Puru wanted us to try chai, the sweet, milky, spicy tea popular throughout India. We watched the chai wallah prepare the drink, heating his spices and milk in a well-used pan balanced over a burner on his metal cart. When it was ready, Puru gave each of us a small, steaming cup of the milky drink, which smelled lovely. I didn't drink mine - cow's milk isn't part of my diet - but one of my fellow travellers happily relieved me of it and knocked it back. "Delicious," she enthused. And then we were off again, shuffling our way along the streets, sweating in the heat.

Eventually I saw daylight at the end of the alleyway and emerged back onto the main road. Puru waited on the street corner while his flock appeared one by one from the crowd, some looking jubilant, others looking battle-worn and dusty, blinking in the bright sunlight after the dimness of the alley. Puru did a headcount then reached into his back pocket for his sunglasses. They'd gone, removed by some light-fingered thief in the crowd. Puru shook his head and laughed. "Wait here," he instructed us, and wandered off. He returned shortly baring a plate of jalebi, which he shared among us. The curly deep-fried treats were soaked in sugar syrup. They were crispy on the outside while soft and chewy on the inside - the perfect treat after our trek through Chandni Chowk.

Jama Masjid

Our next stop was at the Jama Masjid, India's oldest mosque. It was a short walk from the pandemonium of Chandni

Chowk, the streets growing quieter as we moved away from the main shopping area. The mosque, which took six years to build and was completed in 1658, can house up to 25,000 worshipers. It has four towers, two minarets and three gateways, the east of which was intended only for use by members of the royal family. There was no entrance fee to visit the mosque but Puru told us that there was quite a hefty charge to take a camera in. Shoes and bags had to be left outside, and I said I would stand guard over them while Alan went in. Puru accepted this offer gratefully and disappeared into the streets as soon as I was settled on the steps and the others had ascended through the gates of the mosque.

To be honest, I was quite grateful for this opportunity to grab a moment of solitude. I'm used to working at home in peace and quiet with cats lounging around, occasionally demanding cuddles or food. Traversing the congested streets of Old Delhi was great fun, but I was badly in need of a time out.

The sun was setting by the time our party emerged from the mosque and Puru had returned from his wanderings. I suspect he was buying sunglasses to replace the ones he lost in the market. The ladies told me that they had been given long shrouds to wear before entering the mosque, covering up their entire bodies.

I looked at the photos Alan had taken inside the mosque and asked him what he thought of it. "It wasn't as impressive as the places we visited yesterday," he said, shrugging, "but it was worth seeing. The courtyard was huge." The mosque-visitors slowly put their footwear back on and sat down on the steps, some of them looking like they should have joined me for a rest instead of going inside. "OK," said Puru. "Now we're going to the Sikh temple. Follow me and don't get lost." And off we went, back into the busy streets.

Sheeshganj Gurudwara

The Sheeshganj Gurudwara, also known as the Sisganj Gurudwara, was back near Chandni Chowk. Before entering the temple itself Puru took us into the basement, where we took off our dusty footwear and handed them over to the man in the shoe-depository. It would cost us money to get them back upon our return. We then exited the basement and walked a short distance in our bare feet along the grimy streets of Old Delhi before putting on our head coverings and wading through a shallow pool at the bottom of the steps leading up into the temple.

This Sikh temple was built in memory of Guru Tegh Bahadur Sahib Ji, a holy man who was beheaded in 1675 by the Mughal ruler Aurangzeb for protecting the rights of Sikhs and refusing to convert to Islam. The original temple was built in 1783 but the existing buildings weren't erected until 1930. It's a lot bigger on the inside than it looks from the street, with about 250 rooms for people who wish to stay overnight. Worshipers sat in the central hall, where holy scriptures are kept underneath a beautifully ornate canopy.

The temple is home to a community kitchen, where anyone, regardless of faith or caste, is welcome to eat. We were permitted to enter certain areas of the kitchen, which was quite an eye-opener. I volunteer in the kitchen of a homeless shelter in Ottawa, but our kitchen is very different to the one I saw in Delhi. We prepare food on large, spotlessly clean, stainless steel countertops, surrounded by ovens, fridges and sinks. In the Delhi kitchen women sat on the floor around a low marble table rolling out chapattis. These were placed onto a conveyer belt travelling over a hot grill. The vast multitude of cooked chapattis fell off the other end of the belt into a huge basket, ready to be served with the fabulously fragrant lentils being cooked in mega-pans in the next room.

In another part of the kitchen a man was making what

looked like porridge in a wok big enough for a family to take a bath in. The heat in this room was intense and we didn't linger any longer than we had to.

It was around 6:30 in the evening, and I was getting hungry. At home we eat at six so that Alan and I can get out in time for various evening activities. I hoped we would be eating in the temple, especially since the food smelled really good, but Puru obviously had other plans. He escorted us out of the building, back to the shoe depository and then to the train station. The journey back to New Delhi seemed to take forever and I was almost grateful for the other bodies pressing against me, holding me up.

Dinner that evening was in a restaurant about a 10-minute walk from the hotel. Alan and I shared aloo gobi, channa dhal and tarka dhal, washed down with Kingsfisher lager. It was delicious, although to be honest I was so hungry that even if the food had been awful and I would still have eaten every morsel.

Agra

The following day started early, heading off to the train station long before sunrise. Traffic was crazy even in the wee hours of the morning, especially as we neared our destination. There was total gridlock as vehicles went the wrong way down one-way streets, blocked junctions and scraped against each other in the dim light. Our taxi driver was unfazed at first but grew increasingly agitated as time slipped by and we hadn't made any progress. After some shouting at other drivers he edged his way across the line of vehicles and drove like a madman to the station parking lot. We weren't the last to arrive and we huddled with others from our group in the station entrance while we waited for everyone to get there, talking in whispers so as not to disturb the people sleeping on the floor. Some had luggage while others simply lay on blankets laid out on the ground.

When the rest of our party arrived, looking a little anxious as a result of their tardiness, Puru ushered us to the ticket gate and onto the platform where we boarded our waiting train. We had assigned seating, so I settled myself next to the window while Alan sat behind me, chatting to a man on leave from the military who was going home to see his wife and daughters. He obviously adored his little girls, and passed photos over the seatback for me to see. As I handed them back I saw a heated argument going on between some of our group and another set of tourists, who were sitting in the wrong seats and refusing to move. After a lot of hand-waving and cross words, the French tourists reluctantly gave up the seats and left to sit somewhere else. If you're travelling by train in India I strongly recommend booking your tickets in advance and getting assigned seating, even if you have to fight for your seats afterwards.

The train departed and I had a peek at the breakfast the Jivitesh Hotel had packed for us to eat on the train, hoping for samosas or something along those lines. I was very disappointed to see a soggy cheese sandwich made with white bread, a banana, an apple and some orange juice. I tried to pick the cheese off the bread but it seemed to be welded on, so I ate my fruit and called it breakfast. At some point during the three-hour journey a steward brought round complimentary drinks and snacks. The tea was greatly appreciated, and the sight of British McVities digestive biscuits made me laugh. This was followed by a small "meals on wheels" container of vegetable croquettes, peas and fries served with slices of brown bread and ketchup. I was very happy to see something I could eat, as I was quite hungry by this time.

As the steward started collecting trays, I heard Alan ask his neighbour what amount he should give as a tip. "One hundred rupees," came the reply. The army man gave the steward his rupee note, and the steward graciously thanked him. Alan handed over the same amount and received a dirty look in reply. The steward paused, obviously hoping for more, until the army man shooed him away. Special rates for tourists...

The train had been chugging along for quite some time before the sun started to rise over the horizon. We sped past open fields, a few of which still had crops waiting to be harvested. I took photos out of the window, being careful to put my camera down as we approached people squatting by the tracks attending to "personal matters". I'm sure the last thing they wanted was a stupid foreigner photographing them during their bathroom break. I find it awkward enough when the cats follow me into the bathroom, and they don't have cameras.

The Red Fort, Agra

We disembarked in Agra and were met at the station by the drivers who would be with us for most of our trip. They drove something advertised as our "private chartered vehicle", which turned out to be a small coach with working air-conditioning and suspension which had seen better days. Our driver was Madhukar, and he did a good, if sometimes hair-raising, job of getting us from one place to another. He was often joined in the front of the coach by Chitranjan, a charming younger man who made sure there was always chilled water on the bus for us to purchase and offered a helping hand when climbing on and off the vehicle. He had a fabulous smile which rarely left his face. He didn't have a seat as such but spent his time sitting cross-legged on a platform in the front of the coach. Despite the bumps and swerving he never fell over backwards, which I think was quite an achievement.

Our first mission in Agra was to explore the Red Fort, so named because of the red sandstone from which it was built. The entry fee for locals was 20 rupees. Tourists paid 300 rupees (about Can $6 / US $5), which was included in the price of our Intrepid tour. Puru led us over the bridge spanning the huge, empty moat and into the fort under the watchful eyes of two bright green parakeets perched on the wall. This was one of two original moats, the outer of which was filled in and had a road built over it. Later in the day Alan bought a guide book on Agra being sold by one of the persistent street vendors who dogged our steps. This guidebook states that "the ditches were full of dreaded crocodiles and tortoise", which seems like a confusing choice of animals to ward off invaders. The guide book makes for entertaining reading, but I'm not sure how accurate the facts are.

The day was already quite hot as we entered the fort. I stopped in the shade of the entryway, taking in the expanse of what lay before me. The fort was much bigger than I'd expected, and might be better described as a walled city. Only certain parts are open to the public; the rest is used by the military. The original fort dates back to the 1100's and has been owned by numerous leaders over the centuries, falling into disrepair as the years went by. Rebuilding of the fort was ordered by the Mughal Emperor Akbar and took eight years to finish. Constructed using red sandstone from Rajasthan, it was completed in 1573 and was used as a military base as well as a palace.

Akabar's grandson Shah Jahan, the man who built the legendary Taj Mahal, changed the red fort considerably when he demolished some of the old structures and added buildings made of white marble. The Red Fort used to contain five hundred buildings, some of which were demolished by Shah, while others were replaced by barracks when the British inhabited the fort between 1803 and 1862. Only thirty Mughal buildings remain on the south-east side of the fort, one of which had a hole in the wall courtesy of a cannonball fired by the British before their occupancy of the fort.

When Shah was declared to be incompetent and unfit to rule by his son Aurangzeb, he was imprisoned in a marble palace within the Red Fort. According to folklore Shah died on the balcony of his ornate prison, lying in the arms of his daughter and gazing at the Taj Mahal - the mausoleum of his beloved wife. I hope he had a clearer view than we did through the modern-day smog which clouded the skyline.

Kalra's Cottage Industry Rugs

I emerged from the Red Fort feeling a bit overwhelmed by the size of the buildings and the beauty of the inlays and carvings. It really wasn't what I had expected to see in India after hearing so many tales focussing on poverty and squalor. During our taxi trip around Delhi we'd seen children performing handstands at traffic lights who banged on the car windows demanding money. "Don't give them anything," Ajay had instructed us. "The government has programs to get children off the streets and into school. They should be studying, not begging." Puru gave us similar advice when we were accosted by beggars at tourist sites. "They do not need to beg. Don't give them money. They do not need to be on the streets." In contrast, he actively supported touts selling junk to tourists by bringing some of the goods onto our coach before we drove away from sites, checking if anyone had "missed the opportunity to buy them earlier."

Our next stop after the Red Fort was at Kalra's Cottage Industry Rugs, frequented I expect by many tour companies taking people around Agra. I hadn't realised this was on the itinerary and sighed inwardly at the thought of sitting through a high-pressure sales presentation designed to sell overpriced rugs to unwitting foreigners. We were ushered into the store where we were given a talk about Indian rugs, which might have been interesting had I not been so hot, tired and hungry. I looked around at my fellow travellers. A few were listening intently while the majority leaned against walls or perched on stools, looking like I felt. Men sat at looms, quietly working on rugs while we watched.

I struggled to focus as our guide told us about the high

quality of the rugs, the types of knots used and the songs sung by the weavers to make sure they were weaving the correct pattern. Things became a lot more interesting when he handed Shannon a box of matches and invited her to set a partially finished rug on fire. Not one to shirk in her duties, Shannon did her best to burn the rug, which resisted her efforts. "This is a good quality rug," beamed the salesman.

From there we followed him into the basement, which was strewn with rugs. Yarn was stacked on shelves, overflowing onto the floor in heaps. This was where the washed, dried rugs were combed then groomed to separate threads and make the patterns as sharp as possible. It looked like hard work requiring perfect eyesight and probably caused a lot of stiff backs. But the finished rugs were quite splendid.

Our next port of call was, inevitably, the sales room, where hundreds of rugs were rolled and stacked on shelves or against the wall. We were directed to plush couches and served vegetable samosas while the salesman unfurled rug after rug to show us the beauty wrapped within.

"This one is silk, woven in a Persian style." "This beauty is wool, woven in a Moghul design." "Do you like red? This traditional pattern rug comes in many sizes." "You like big rugs? Take off your shoes and walk on this one! Feel how soft it is on your feet!" "Our rugs are very hard-wearing. They don't give friction burns. Resistant to stains. Good for children!" After we finished our very-welcome snacks we all took off our shoes and walked around on the beautiful carpets, oohing and aahing where required. Then Alan made a fatal error. "How much is this one?" he asked, pointing to a 3ft x 5ft green rug. His personal assistant was eager to supply the information, pointing out that the prices were set and nonnegotiable, but that the government would pay for the rug to be shipped anywhere in the world. As I wandered over to have a look I heard a "pop" and we were plunged into darkness.

This had obviously happened before, judging from the speed with which the salesmen conjured up torches without pausing in their patter. "What do you think" Alan asked me, pointing to his favourite rug. "How much?" I asked, preparing myself to hear a high number. I wasn't disappointed. "Wow. That's a lot of money for a rug, even with free shipping to Canada." But it was beautiful. It was hand-made. It would always remind us of our trip to India, bought in Agra on Alan's birthday. There was a spot on our bedroom floor in need of a rug. And so, by the light of a torch, Alan signed the back of the carpet and handed over his credit card. Part of me feared that we would never see the rug again, but five weeks after returning home it was delivered safe and sound, and, I have to say, it looks beautiful in our bedroom.

It's the favourite place for our 24lb cat to take an afternoon nap, making me grateful that it's as durable as the salesman promised.

The Taj Mahal

Madhukar dropped us off at our hotel to freshen up and grab lunch at the buffet before we continued our adventures. The Howard Plaza Hotel was located in the middle of town, the entry guarded by a doorman with a fabulous moustache. I believe it was here that Lily started her collection of decorative facial hair photos in India, using her abundant charm to get photos of even the most reluctant moustached gentlemen. Our room was lovely, and the teabags next to a kettle were a welcome sight. The bathroom was separated from the bedroom by a floor-to-ceiling window, which fortunately could be covered with a blind when the toilet was in use. Alan and I have been together for a long time but there are still some activities we don't wish to have an audience for.

The hotel was only a short drive from our next destination - the famous "teardrop on the face of eternity". There can't be many people who haven't heard the story behind the Taj Mahal, which was built by the fifth Moghul emperor Shah Jahan after the death of his beloved wife Arjuman Banu Begum, whom Shah called Mumtaz Mahal - "Chosen One of the Palace". Unlike his other wives, Mumtaz was Shah's companion during his military campaigns and carried his imperial seal. She died in 1631 while giving birth to their thirteenth child and was placed in a temporary grave in Burhanpur, where her body rested until Shah completed his military campaign. She was later carried in a gold coffin to Agra where for 22 years she lay in a building by the banks of the river while the Taj was constructed by 20,000 workers from across northern India. The central marble-domed mausoleum was the first building to be completed, followed by the red sandstone buildings, pool and gardens. Often portrayed as a tranquil place to sit and contemplate the wonders of love, this tribute to Mumtaz Mahal is considered to be an essential part of any tour of northern India.

The Taj was one of the few places during our tour where we were free to wander at will, unescorted by an (often verbose) local guide. "Come back after the sun goes down and meet here on the street," Puru told us. "You have to see reflections in the pool at sunset before you leave." With these rather vague instructions in mind, Alan and I held hands and prepared for the most romantic day of our lives. The sun was shining, it was Alan's birthday and we were going to see the sunset at the Taj Mahal. Can you imagine anything more romantic than that?

It soon became obvious that this was not going to be the romantic encounter of my dreams. Princess Diana sat in solitude by the pool of the Taj many years ago without another soul in sight, but my experience could not have been more different. I had by now resigned myself to being followed by people taking photographs of me and Alan, but nothing could have prepared me for the onslaught of photographers hounding the two of us as we walked towards the entrance of the Taj Mahal. Some were "professional" photographers who were chased away by the one assigned to our group by Puru. "Only let this man take your photos. He will meet you outside when you leave for you to buy your pictures. Don't give money to anyone else." The others brandishing cameras were Indian tourists, all wanting a picture of Ali Baba and his wife. When we posed for our "official" photograph by the pool in front of the Taj our photographer had to repeatedly shoo others out of the way so that he could do his work. The pictures we bought from him were all slightly crooked, but at least they didn't have other people in the middle of the frame with us.

Once the photography session was over Alan and I began our journey towards the famous mausoleum. Our steps were slow, not because we were savouring the beauty of the gardens but because people kept jumping in front of us, brandishing their cameras. I tried to be kind, but there's a limit to how often I can smile and look sincere. We were being hounded by a large group of young men when a security guard pushed his way through. "Are they bothering you?" he growled. I didn't want to get them in trouble with this fierce looking man, so I told him everything was fine. "It's not fine," he said. "Foreign visitors are very important. YOU (he waved his hands at the young men) LEAVE THEM ALONE!" The young men looked totally deflated, so I suggested that we do a group shot and then they had to leave us in peace. The guard nodded his assent and let them take a number of photos before bellowing "Enough!" He gave Alan a nod before marching away. The young men thanked us then dispersed, and for the remainder of our visit we were left in relative peace.

After taking some time to admire the pools and lush green lawns, Alan and I made our way to the mausoleum, dismayed to see the huge line of people waiting to go up the steps to the marble courtyard in front of the tomb. A guard approached us. "You want to go in?" he asked. Alan nodded. "This way," the guard said, pointing to a sign hanging on the wall. We thanked him, put the disposable covers Puru had given us over our shoes, and climbed the marble stairs. Indian people paid 20 rupees for their tickets whereas ours cost 750 rupees. It was almost worth the extra money to avoid waiting in an unbelievably long line to enter the tomb of Mumtaz Mahal.

The inside of the dark mausoleum was crowded with people, packed tightly together and shuffling around the octagonal inner chamber. Guards blew loud whistles and shouted warnings over the sounds of feet on the marble. "No talking. No photographs. Keep moving." An intricately carved marble screen surrounded the two sarcophagi in the middle of room, which were decorated with beautiful inlays. I was disappointed to learn later that these were not the real tombs of Shah Jahan and his beloved Mumtaz Mahal, which lie in the basement hidden from view from the thousands of tourists flocking into the mausoleum each year. I emerged blinking into the bright sunlight and waited for Alan to reappear, relieved to have some personal space after the congestion within. A monkey perching on the wall watched her companions play below in the courtyard of a red sandstone mosque, oblivious to the tourists flocking by.

Alan emerged from the tomb looking slightly dazed but otherwise happy. "That was quite an experience," he said with a smile. I couldn't have agreed more. We walked down the marble steps, put our shoe coverings into a waiting garbage can and spent a few moments sitting by the pool before heading towards the mosque. When we got there we realised we'd made a mistake when we threw away the shoe covers. Shoes were not allowed in the mosque unless covered, and Puru had warned us about leaving our shoes anywhere. "Indian people's shoes will be there when they return but if you leave your shoes somewhere they will vanish." Bother. I elected to look after Alan's shoes while he went in, happy to spend some time just sitting quietly with my thoughts.

The crowds were thinning rapidly as the sun started to set, making it seem almost peaceful. When Alan came out of the mosque we returned to the pool in front of the Taj Mahal and settled down to wait for the reflections to appear. It was worth the wait as the image of the beautiful building appeared in the still waters of the pool. We jostled with other tourists as one by one we took postcard-worthy photos of "the Jewel of Muslim Art in India."

Dinner that evening was served at tables on a treed patio with fairy lights. Musicians played traditional instruments as we ordered our meals. Lucinda and Linus ordered the vegetarian tandoori platter, on a personal mission to order the same dish everywhere we went. Sometimes their meal arrived, sometimes it didn't, but they enjoyed themselves regardless. When we'd all finished dining the musicians struck up an Indian adaptation of "happy birthday" as Puru brought in a large chocolate birthday cake for Alan. It was a lovely gesture and Alan smiled happily as he was bestowed with a garland of flowers and had a lucky string tied around his wrist. He wore it throughout the tour and it now hangs on the bedpost back home. Sometimes he gets lucky.

Jaipur

After an early breakfast we piled into our coach to start our journey towards Jaipur, the capital of Rajasthan. By now we had all chosen our seats for the trip, and Alan and I were lucky enough to secure ones in the middle of the vehicle where the bouncing was least pronounced. Not far behind us sat Jasmina, who was coughing up quite a storm. I felt badly for her – it's no fun being ill on holiday. By the end of the tour most of us, through no fault on Jasmina's part, succumbed to the virus to one extent or another, dosing ourselves with medications bought from dusty hole-in-the-wall pharmacies our coach driver stopped at from time to time. I'd brought numerous medications with me, but flu treatments were among those left at home. If only I'd known that shots given in Canada don't prevent one from catching an Australian flu bug in India…

We took a toll road from Agra to our first stop of the day at Fatehpur Sikri, marvelling at the random cars travelling the wrong way along our side of the divided highway. Madhukar sped along merrily, honking frequently and swerving when needed to avoid cows, donkeys and oncoming traffic. There were occasional squeals from someone in our midst who eventually came to accept what the rest of us already knew. Our driver had grown up on the streets of India and was unlikely to mow down cattle or run over a motorcycle as he did the Indian-drivers-dance along the highway. And while the one and a half-hour trip to Fatehpur Sikri was quite exciting at times, we all arrived intact.

Fatehpur Sikri

To get to the city of Fatehpur Sikri itself, we had to leave our large coach and board a smaller one which took us up to the site. As we walked from one vehicle to the other we were mobbed by men selling jewellery. They soon realised that their best chances of getting a sale were the younger ladies in our group, especially Lily and Angie. Lily was a natural flirt and managed to smile sweetly while being pressured to buy the "beautiful bracelets for a beautiful lady." She gave in and bought an ankle bracelet, thinking they would then leave her alone. She couldn't have been more wrong. Buying one was not enough. "Buy one for your other ankle." "Buy one for your friend." "I give you good price for five!" Even after we boarded the small coach the bartering continued, with hands waving bracelets through the open windows. There was an audible sigh of relief from the ladies when we set off, leaving the jewellery men standing in a cloud of dust.

The red sandstone city of Fatehpur Sikri was built by the Mughal Emperor Jalal-ud-din Mohammad Akbar and blends together Islamic and Hindu architecture. Surrounded by an 11km-long wall with numerous gates, the city contains a large mosque, a palace complex and a marble tomb built for the Sufi saint Salim Christi. Most of the gardens and buildings were constructed between 1571 and 1585. It was abandoned shortly after Akbar died when a lack of water made life there unsustainable. Fatehpur Sikri has a huge courtyard just inside the tourist gate and it was here Akbar held court with his advisors, the acoustics making it possible to hear everything that was said within the courtyard. According to our guide, convicted criminals were executed in the courtyard by being trampled to death by elephants. He pointed out an indentation where the prisoners placed their heads so that the elephants could stamp on them, which was really rather gruesome. A much more pleasant sight was the Diwan-i-Khas (Hall of Private Audiences), located at the end of the courtyard. An impressively massive stone pillar stood in the center of the room, supporting four bridges linking the corners of the balcony.

Other buildings in the courtyard included the treasury and a small palace which some say was built for Akbar's Turkish Muslim wife. A much larger building was the Panch Mahal, a five story pavilion built so that each story was smaller than the one below it. To one side of the courtyard sat a rather murky ornamental pool with a central platform on which musicians used to perform for Akbar.

Our guide also showed us the palace of Akbar's favourite wife, the Hindu lady Jodh Bai. It sat on a large courtyard next to the palace of Akbar's third wife, Miriam. There is some debate about Miriam's religion, some saying she was a Goan Christian and others arguing that Akbar didn't have a Christian wife. The palace itself is a mixture of Islamic and Hindu designs, with a vast array of geometric patterns from the former mingling with the flowers and butterflies of the latter. It was quite beautiful and must have been even more impressive when the city was inhabited.

We left the courtyard and entered the huge mosque, which required us to deposit our shoes outside the gate and pay to get them back when we left. Ryan and Linus were wearing shorts and had to cover their legs with black skirts provided by the mosque. I'm not sure it's a fashion statement either of them would be recreating when they got home, but I thought they both looked fabulous.

The white marble tomb of Shaikir Salim Chishti is located in the courtyard of the mosque. The outside is constructed from intricately carved lattice screens on which childless women tie threads, hoping it will help them to conceive. According to legend Akbhar himself was childless until he was blessed by the saint, after which he fathered three sons. Inside the tomb I could see a gilded canopy over a bed covered with brightly coloured silks, around which worshipers walked silently. Shaikh Salim Chishti's family lie in a graveyard outside his tomb next to a barred gate leading to an underground tunnel which is said to go all the way to Agra.

This tour seemed to go on forever. Our local guide was a nice man who had a lot of information to impart, but after an early start and a long drive it was hard to appreciate standing around under the hot sun listening to him talk. I would have been much happier wandering around on my own, taking considerably less time to see the abandoned city than the tour took. I'm pleased we went there, and it broke up the journey from Agra to Jaipur, but I wasn't sorry to leave. We bought our shoes back and headed off to the waiting coach, where we were delayed until Lily and Angie navigated their way through men selling an assortment of tourist junk. In the parking lot where we would transfer back onto our usual coach sat a snake charmer, who was happy to let us all take his picture in return for money. I have to say that the snakes didn't look particularly "charmed", especially the large one he held in one hand while playing his pipe with the other, but as far as I could tell they looked healthy and well-fed. Not that I went too close.

I'd just settled into my seat on the coach when I felt something bite my chest. I looked down my t-shirt and saw a pink inch-long earwig-like insect gripping my flesh between two large pincers. I let out a squeal and rummaged through my pockets for a tissue with which to grab the beast. Alan looked at me in surprise as I flapped around and then shoved a tissue down my front. I gave the beastie a big squeeze and yanked it off, then opened the tissue to show Alan. "Wow," he said "Was that down your t-shirt?" I had puncture holes where the insect had attached itself which were beginning to swell. Alan dug alcohol wipes out of my purse and I was grateful for the after-bite Beth handed to me. Puru wandered down the coach to see what all the fuss was about, and took away my squashed insect with a laugh and a shrug. "You won't die from this," he chortled.

The next item on our agenda for the day was lunch, and we took a brief detour up the wrong side of highway in order to get there. One pot of tea, a stuffed vegetarian paratha and a vegetable curry later I was ready to climb back on the coach and nap away part of three hour journey to Jaipur. We passed by farmhouses with thatched roofs, tiny villages with market stalls, stonemasons selling carved statues of elephants and cannons, and toll booths where men sold bags of peanuts to drivers waiting to go through.

And So To Bed

Eventually our coach dropped us off at our hotel in Jaipur. The website promised "eco-friendly travel with easy access to Jaipur's forts, palaces and bazaars." It went on to say "Devraj Niwas has 21 elegantly-designed rooms with a mix of handcrafted antique and modern furniture. The well-furnished accommodation blends nature with contemporary design, providing unmatched comfort and adding to the calm ambiance with style. The tropical plants at Devraj Niwas create mini-courtyards giving peace and privacy to each room." It was a very pretty place to stay, with the promised plants looking lush and green. Winding pathways led from the main building to small rows of private rooms, and I only took a wrong turning once or twice. Our room contained a comfortable bed and some old wooden furniture. The attached bathroom had a shower, sink and western-style toilet. Much to my amusement the light was lashed together with tape, wires clearly visible through the hole in the plaster. The accommodation was basic but comfortable and it was nice to take a hot shower to wash off the day's dirt before dinner.

The outdoor dining room of the hotel looked beautiful under the dark sky. Candles were burning brightly and a fire extinguisher hung from a tree in case the flames became too big. Our group bought drinks from the central bar, then settled down to a dinner of delicious Indian food. We'd almost finished when the sky was filled with sparkling fireworks. "There's a wedding palace next door," Puru explained. "You can go and see if you want, but be careful of the fireworks." We all rushed down the garden path in time to see a beautiful silver carriage go by in which the groom sat on a high seat with a woman and girls sitting at his feet.

Men walked before and after the carriage carrying huge candelabras on their heads, powered by a generator bringing up the rear. A marching band walked along, music filling the air as crowds of beautifully dressed men, women and children filed past. We joined the end of the procession, being careful to avoid the boxes of fireworks being set off in the middle of the busy road, the owners apparently unaware of the passing traffic.

The procession entered the grounds of the wedding palace, where a party was taking place. Lily took pictures of some fabulous moustaches for her collection, taking particular note of an elderly gentleman in a splendid red and white tunic, white pants, curly-toed red shoes and a bright red turban. “He says we’re all invited to the party,” she said enthusiastically. Alan and I felt that we had intruded enough and quietly left, followed shortly by the others. I’ve no doubt that we would have been made very welcome at the party, but we could hear our beds calling us over sound of the music.

The Wind Palace

After a breakfast of lentil curry and deep-fried bread (yes, I put on weight in India) we set off on our adventures for the day. Our first stop was on a busy street to see the Wind

Palace. This beehive-like structure was built by the Maharaja Sawai Pratap Singh in 1799 so that his wives could see the activities taking place on the street without revealing their faces. The top three stories are the thickness of a single room. There are courtyards, which we didn't get to see, behind the palace. It was difficult to get good pictures of the building, located as it is on a road, but the best vantage point was from an island in the middle of the traffic. I was content to stand and look up at the windows while Alan took his life in his hands and bolted through the traffic, walking along the central island until he could fit most of the palace into his shot. Thanks Hon.

The Amber Fort

We walked down the street, passing by stores selling the usual tourist souvenir t-shirts, parasols and fridge magnets, and boarded the coach. It wasn't long before we reached the Amber Fort, also known as Amer Fort, which we could see perched high on a hill, shining in the sunlight beneath crystal clear skies. It was immense, stretching across the horizon and reflecting in Maota Lake below. I peered up at the fort wall, realising that it was going to be quite a trek to get up there under the blazing sun, but I figured if the Aunties could make it I could too. They were probably 20 years older than me and very sprightly, but they too were looking at the winding pathways with frowns on their faces.

Puru led us across the road and we started our ascent up some steps which seemed to go on forever. We stopped periodically "to look at the view" and let stragglers catch up, fending off the perpetually-invasive souvenirs-sellers. "You want nice umbrella to keep sun away? Look - many pretty colours. I do you good deal for two." And then we were off again, climbing ever higher step by step by step.

About halfway through our climb we crossed over a wide paved road. "Keep out of the way of the elephants," Puru warned us. "They won't stop to let you cross the road." Before we'd started our walk up the hill Puru had told us that there were about 80 elephants at Amber Fort who were used to carry tourists. "Elephants were not made to walk on concrete," he said emphatically. "The road hurts their feet and they should not be used in this way. They work very hard and don't get enough rest. We will be walking up and will not support this treatment of the elephants." We all nodded our agreement. When the elephants passed us on the road they looked tired and sad, despite the brightly coloured paint on their skin. One owner hit his elephant with a stick when she slowed down as she walked by. The elephants are treated much better now than they were in years gone by, but things are still far from perfect. The Jaipur government has placed restrictions limiting each animal to five trips per day carrying only two tourists up the hill each time and do routine inspections to make sure the elephants are in good health. Hopefully one day they will ban the use of elephants at the Amber Fort.

We arrived at the Surya Pole (the main entrance) and passed through the huge gateway into the first courtyard of the fort, hot, tired and slightly jubilant after our trek. While some of us stood waiting for the last ones to arrive, a salesman approached us holding a copy of a newspaper. "Are any of you British?" he asked with a huge grin. We all turned to look at Lily. The man held up the paper and laughed loudly. "Then you are very lazy!" he announced before shaking the paper at her and walking away.

Once we had all arrived we were introduced to our local guide, a fount of knowledge who would impart all kinds of wisdom to us during our visit. I groaned inwardly, having already had my fill of verbose guides for one trip. On a good day I have the attention span of a three-year-old and find it very hard to listen to anyone for more than five minutes. Fortunately Alan is a much better listener than I am, so while I wandered taking photos he stood and listened, telling me edited highlights as we moved from place to place.

Construction of the Amber Fort was started by Raja Bihar Singh in 1552 and added to by his successors over a period of many years. The palaces were built around four courtyards set on different levels. The first of these, the Jaleb Chowk, was where soldiers gathered. Steps from this courtyard lead into the palace through the Ganesh Pol, a beautiful three-story gate.

The Diwan-i-aam or Hall of Public Audience is in the second courtyard. It was here that the Raja sat to hear petitions from the local people, surrounded by the many columns supporting the roof.

We accessed the private quarters of the Maharaja and his family through the Ganesh Pol. The third courtyard contained a lush green garden built on platforms, decorated with pools and fountains. It was built according to a traditional Mughal design incorporating hexagons, narrow channels lined with marble and a star-shaped pool with a fountain at the center.

A woman wearing a beautiful bright yellow sari

worked quietly in the gardens, ignoring the many tourists asking her to look up and smile for the camera. In her hand she held a broom made of sticks tied together on a long handle, and she had better things to do than stop working to pose for a picture or two.

Two buildings faced each other across the third courtyard. The Jai Mandir (Hall of Victory) is decorated with a multitude of inlaid glass pieces and small mirrors. It's also known as the Sheesh Mahal (Mirror Palace) and is said to resemble a glittering jewel box when illuminated with candles.

Across from the Mirror Palace lies the Hall of Pleasure (Sukh Mahal). Piped water runs through a channel in this building, acting as an air conditioning system.

Sitting proudly on top of a hill behind the Hall of Pleasure we could see Jaipur Fort, which is connected to the Amber Fort by underground tunnels. It was to here that the

Maharaja and his family would retreat in times of unrest.

To the south of this garden courtyard lies the oldest part of the fort. The Palace of Man Singh I took twenty-five years to build and was completed in 1599. A pavilion sits in the middle of this courtyard, which was adorned with curtains when it was used for private meetings between the women of the royal family.

The Amber Fort was enormous and the tour seemed to go on for much longer than anyone in the group would have liked on such a hot day. We all carried water with us, but it was still draining to stand around under the blazing sun for a few hours. By the time our guide finally handed us back to Puru we were all rather subdued. "Did you enjoy the tour?" he asked. "Yes, it was great," came the mumbled reply as people shuffled back down the hillside to our waiting coach. I expected that our next stop would be somewhere for lunch, forgetting that Indian mealtimes and Canadian ones are not the same thing. Instead our coach took us along a wide, busy street where we paused briefly to look at the Jal Mahal (Water Palace) sitting in a lake, partially hidden in the haze rising from the water.

From there we were driven to "Jewels N Arts" where we were invited to look at their gemstones and be astonished by their prices. I'm not a "sparkly" kind of girl and settled down on one of the couches while others looked for gifts for loved ones or for themselves. The salesmen tried numerous times to engage Alan in conversations about buying something for his lovely wife before realising that I really didn't want anything.

They changed their tactics. "Do you wear shirts, Sir? Look at these beautiful cuff links. You can't find anything like this in Canada, especially for this price." They were right about the price, which was outrageous. Alan shook his head. "I already have some," he replied. The salesman's eyes lit up, obviously thinking he'd got a sure sale now that Alan had admitted to wearing cufflinks. "Perhaps these would be more to your liking," he said, showing Alan some cufflinks set with unusual purple and green stones. They were quite beautiful. Alan looked at me for approval and I gave him a slight nod. For the right price they would be something I could see him wearing. "How much are they?" The reply made me snort. There's no way anyone in their right mind would pay that much for them. Alan made a counter offer and it was the salesman's turn to snort. "I can tell you don't really want them," he said, putting them back in the display case. Alan shrugged and joined me on the couch.

A few minutes passed before the salesman tried again. His proposal was slightly lower than his first price but still more than we would consider paying. Alan countered with slightly more than his first offer. "That's as high as I'm willing to go. If they're more than that I won't buy them." Again the cufflinks went back into the display case. By now everyone else was paying for their purchases and getting ready to leave. Alan and I stood and started towards the door. The salesman saw his last chance to make a sale and took it. "OK. I'll sell them to you for what you offered. But you are breaking my heart. So little money for something so beautiful." Alan left with a lovely pair of cufflinks, secure in the knowledge that he'd still paid the "special price for tourists".

Jantar Mantar Observatory

After a lunch of spiced lentils and rice, I felt ready for the rest of the day's adventures. I eagerly climbed back into the coach which drove along the streets of Jaipur and deposited us next to some cows in the middle of the city. One of them seemed to take a particular liking to Alan, making me think that perhaps her owner also had a red beard.

We didn't have far to walk, passing t-shirt stalls and people selling fruits and vegetables, before we arrived at our destination - the Jantar Mantar Observatory. One of five open-air observatories built in India by King Jai Singh II, this is home to nineteen astronomical instruments built in the 18th century to observe the movement of celestial bodies with the naked eye. It was the last one to be constructed and is the best preserved. Restoration work took place in the early 1900's, turning it into one world's best collections of pre-telescopic stone instruments in functioning condition. Some measure local time while others look at the stars and constellations.

As we toured the site it was one of the few places in Rajasthan where I actually appreciated having a knowledgeable guide, even though I can't claim to have understood much of what he said about the instruments on display.

Our first port of call was a large, sundial-like structure, where our guide asked us to work out what time the instrument said it was. He then asked us to look at our watches and cell phones. The sundial appeared to be off by exactly seven minutes. Our guide was delighted. "That's because the sundial shows the local time for Jaipur, not the standard Indian international time-zone time displayed on your cell phones, and it's accurate to within twenty seconds."

From there we moved on to the Jaiprakesh Yantra, consisting of two discs set into the ground. Astronomers can stand inside the discs and use inverted maps of the sky created in the marble to track the movements of the sun and other celestial bodies.

Near the Jaiprakesh Yantra were the twelve structures of the Rasivalaya Yantra, which together function as one instrument. Each component is related to a particular sign of the zodiac and becomes operative when the sign of the zodiac it represents approaches the meridian.

After stopping at numerous other instruments we made our way to the Vrihat Samrat Yantra, the world's largest gnomon (sun-casting) sundial. This enormous structure is 88 feet (27 metres) tall and measures time in intervals of 2 seconds. The top platform was used to make announcements to the local people about solar eclipses or the imminent arrival of monsoons.

After our tour we were free to wander for a while, shaking our heads in wonder at the accuracy of large astrological devices built so long ago. There were signs in English next to each of the instruments, but they weren't particularly helpful since I don't know what words such as "digamsa," "azimuth," "pals" or "ghatis" mean. Perhaps I should have paid more attention during our guided tour.

We returned to the hotel for dinner (curry, of course) before heading out for a night at the movies. The ladies in the group dressed up for the event, wearing tunics and long pants with bindi stuck in the middle of our foreheads. I wore a pantsuit bought from the store our taxi driver took Alan and I to in Delhi when we first arrived in India. I'd wanted to buy something saffron or bright orange, but the only items the sales assistant would give me to try on were beige with purple, brown or black accents. "Better for a married woman," he insisted. I eventually bought a beige top with a black paisley print and a few sparkles, along with black patterned pants and a scarf. The colour didn't suit me and the cut made me look like I was the size of a house but it was lightweight, easy to pack and comfortable. I wore it a few times during the trip and smiled sweetly when people told me how lovely I looked, knowing that they were just being kind.

We saw the movie at the beautiful art deco style Raj Mandir cinema, the construction of which began in 1966 and took ten years to complete.

We bought popcorn in the lobby and climbed the stairs to our comfortable seats on the back row of the balcony. The lights dimmed and the film started, accompanied by cheers and clapping from the auditorium below us. The romantic comedy "Happy New Year" was great fun and easy to follow even though it was in Hindi with no subtitles. There was dancing and fighting, a drug heist and a dance competition, buff men and beautiful women. A health warning appeared on the screen every time alcohol was served in the movie. I smiled until my face ached. I couldn't believe it when most of our tour group left at the intermission and were put into tuk-tuks by Puru to make their way back to the hotel. Only Alan, Lily, Ryan, Puru and I remained. After the diamonds had been successfully stolen, the dance competition won and the final credits had rolled, four of us stuffed ourselves into a tuk-tuk and headed for home, tired but laughing all the way.

Mandawa

The following morning we piled onto the coach and headed off towards Mandawa, known as a great place to see beautifully decorated havelis (houses). It's a remote town in the Shekhawati region of Rajasthan which was on the ancient caravan route between China and the Middle East. Some of the havelis are well preserved while others have fallen into a state of disrepair, but the town is basically a large open-air museum. It's about a five-hour drive from Jaipur to Mandawa, so Puru organised a trip to a pharmacy before we'd gone too far to help reduce the amount of coughing taking place on the coach. The flu bug was making its way through the group, although Alan and I were lucky and had resisted it so far. The pharmacist handed out cold and flu medications, and doled out antibiotics to anyone who wanted them, no prescriptions needed. A few members of the group also bought tummy meds to combat the effects of eating curry for lunch, breakfast, dinner and snacks.

Asha Ka Jharna

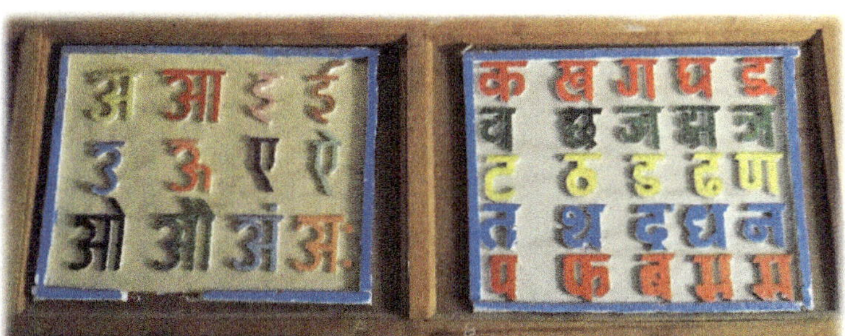

We'd travelled for about two and a half hours before stopping at the village of Nawalgarh to visit the Asha Ka Jharna School for special needs children. The non-profit organisation has three schools which provide services for children and adults with disabilities. At the location we visited there are about one hundred and sixty children receiving special or vocational education, guidance and counselling.

We were met in the office by the principal of the school and were served tea while we learned about the foundation and the work they do. We were then given a tour to see the facilities and watch activities taking place in the classrooms. I felt a bit uncomfortable at first with the idea of the children "performing" for us until a teacher explained that they have many visitors and the children enjoy showing off the things they've achieved. Some of the younger students demonstrated how they could put shapes into the correct size hole in a puzzle board, while older students demonstrated their math skills on a chalkboard. The school was a cheerful place, with bright blue doors and pictures painted on the ceilings. The playground had a couple of swings and they had a computer room where games were used to help children enhance their reading skills.

Before we left we were invited to buy products made by the school to raise funds. I couldn't resist buying the hardback cookbook even though it added weight to my backpack. I find it easy to resist the temptation of diamonds and sparkly gemstones, but cookbooks? I'm an easy target.

Lunch was a short drive away, travelling along country roads and taking occasional detours when the road was blocked by broken-down vehicles. Some of the fields were full of crops but many lay empty, the crop already harvested. We stopped at the Shekhawati guest house for a buffet lunch made with organic produce. The spiced baby eggplants were fabulous served with yellow lentils, rice, cauliflower with potatoes and deep-fried bread. A pet cat sat on the low wall of the outdoor dining room with her back to us, more interested in the antics of the dogs than she was in us. And then it was back into the coach for the remainder of our trip to Mandawa, trying to nap while listening to the sounds of people coughing.

Desert Resort Hotel Mandawa

We eventually pulled into the parking lot of the resort we where would be staying while visiting Mandawa. Situated down a long, dusty road, it certainly earned the name of a *desert* resort. The tourist information described it as having "unusual architecture ... recreated in the style of a typical Rajasthani village". It was certainly interesting to look at and appeared to be constructed out of mud, but maybe it was mud-coloured concrete. Alan said it made him think of the African plains and he half expected to see a lion or two lurking behind the bushes or an elephant taking a dip in the pool.

The complex contained numerous small, round huts with thatched roofs along with a courtyard surrounded by adjoining rooms, which is where we would be sleeping. It was quite different to any of the places we'd stayed so far, and when I was shown to the room Alan and I would be sharing I really wasn't sure I liked it. It was very dimly lit and the small windows were covered with thick fabric hangings. I peeked out of the rear window and glimpsed a gloomy dirt courtyard. Everything looks much brighter and more welcoming in the photos than it did in real life. Metal rings hung from the concrete ceiling above the concrete bed, which was topped with a thin mattress and looked like it might be a bit on the hard side. It was. At one end of the room was an area with two chairs and a table next to a concrete "sofa" topped with cushions. The most bizarre part of the suite was the bathroom. The two huge wooden doors leading into the bathroom had a lock on the outside rather than on the inside. The shower, which had hot water intermittently, was surrounded by a curtain but wasn't set into a base of any kind. The shower water flooded the bathroom and then slowly drained away, making visits to the toilet quite a wet affair.

I freshened up and went to join the rest of our group on the rooftop to watch the sun set over the desert. It would have been much pleasanter had a group of German tourists not kept "shushing" us as they tried to listen to their tour guide tell them about the resort. We'd seen them at other tourist sites and they didn't seem very friendly, making me appreciate my own group all the more. A small bar on the rooftop was staffed by a couple of gentlemen wearing brightly coloured turbans. It wasn't long before Lily had sweet-talked one of them into removing their headgear and placing it on her head as she posed behind the bar. We all laughed loudly as the sun sank under the horizon, aware of the disapproving glares coming from the Germans but having too much fun to care.

We retired to the restaurant to have dinner, which was over-priced and not the best food we had on the trip, before the special event of the evening. We were directed towards plastic chairs positioned on a lawn in front of a small stage decorated with curtains and illuminated by a few lights, and when everyone was settled, the show began. Kathputi is a traditional Rajasthan puppet show with a long history dating back thousands of years. It's very popular in the region and no village fair or religious festival is complete without a puppet show. This was a one-man show, the puppeteer speaking in squeaky voices through a bamboo reed while his puppets danced and sang. It was quite entertaining and unlike any puppet show I'd ever seen before. We were invited to buy some puppets after the show, but I'm not sure any of us did so before either heading off to bed or meeting at the ping-pong table for a game or two before retiring for the night.

The Havelis of Mandawa

The following morning we took a short coach ride into the center of Mandawa for a guided tour of the havelis for which the town is famous. Madhukar dropped us off at a street market, the road lined with vendors selling fruits, vegetables, large wok-like pans and other assorted goods. Cows wandered at will among the stalls and traffic, seeming to stop and look at wares in store windows. The roads, buildings and cows were covered in dust, looking dingy and grey in contrast with the brightly coloured saris of ladies shopping at the stalls. There was quite a variety of vegetables available for sale, some of which I recognised while others were unfamiliar. Street food was being cooked on rickety wagons, flies sitting on the ingredients doing whatever it is that flies do to pass the time away.

We wandered the streets for the next couple of hours, stopping from time to time while our guide pointed out painted walls and homes. The colours shone brightly in the sun under the clear blue skies and must have looked splendid when they were first painted.

We stopped at one of the restored havelis, which is open to the public as well as being a family home. Puppies lazed around on a porch near their drinking bowl, poking each other occasionally and nibbling each other's ears. Entrance to the courtyard was through a large gate, hiding the paintings on the haveli walls from the outside world. Many havelis in Rajasthan have two courtyards, the outer one used by men and an inner, secluded one for women.

There was a gift shop at the final haveli we visited, although I use the term loosely. It was more like a junk shop, with dust-covered papers, clothes and knickknacks lying around in heaps. Ryan found an old metal helmet with a large spike on top and a chain mail veil, which he a modelled for us out in the courtyard, looking fierce in a hot, dusty, Irish kind of way.

Back on the main street, we sat in the central courtyard of Mandawa Haveli Hostel for lunch. The deep-fried pakoras were hot, crispy, unhealthy and delicious. Afterwards we boarded the coach for the return trip to the resort, delayed slightly by some intrepid explorers who wanted to sample the potato-stuffed peppers being fried up on a cart. We'd been advised not to eat street food, and when asked the following day how their tummies were the pepper-eaters were strangely silent.

An Afternoon of "Relaxation"

The afternoon was free for us to enjoy relaxing at the desert resort, swimming in the pool or purchasing one of the therapeutic treatments available in the spa. Alan and I were feeling the effects of riding around in a coach with minimal suspension and decided to treat ourselves to a massage, picturing soft beds, plush pillows, relaxing music and maybe some hot stones. On our way to our appointment we passed someone who had just had a massage. "How was it?" I asked. She paused, obviously trying to find the right words to describe her experience. "Different." She shook her head and continued on her way. Alan and I looked at each other, unsure of what this meant, and then climbed the stairs into the massage center.

Ayurveda is one of the world's oldest holistic healing

systems and has been used in India for thousands of years. It's based on the belief that creating balance between mind, body and spirit is essential for good health. As I sat on a cold plastic chair in the corridor of a mud hut, I wasn't sure that any of the three - mind, body or spirit - were feeling particularly happy. A door opened and a lady beckoned me into a small room with a high glassless window, a couple of hooks on the wall and a central concrete slab topped with a very thin plastic-covered pad. She gestured for me to undress completely and hang my clothes on the hooks. I looked around for towels or something to wrap around me for a modicum of decency, but nothing was to be found. The "strip naked and lie on this slab" approach was far removed from my usual spa experiences, but it was too late to turn and run.

I spent the next 45 minutes face down on the slab, a towel folded up under my forehead, covered in goosebumps thanks to the cold draft coming in through the window. The massage was... thorough. Never before have my buttocks been handled so vigorously. My shoulders were de-knotted with determination. My calves were pummeled to the point where I thought I may never walk again. The masseuse was skilled and very strong, and she obviously knew what she was doing. But the whole experience was not what I would describe as pleasant or relaxing, and it was quite a relief when it was all over and I could roll off the slab to get dressed.

I was finished a few minutes before Alan, so I was able to see his face as he emerged from his mud cell. I think "shell-shocked" best describes his expression. We walked back to our room in silence, both processing our experiences before sharing them. After showering off the oils I asked him how his massage had been. "It was a very… different," he started slowly, thoughtfully. "I was lying stark naked face up on a concrete bed while a strange man rubbed the top of my inner thigh. It was very… odd." We shared our experiences over dinner with others who had been for various treatments, and I realised we'd actually got off quite lightly. Three people had elected for the sinus cleanse, hoping it would help rid them of the flu bug. To say they didn't enjoy it is a bit of an understatement, but inhaling vapours, snorting oils and having their nasal cavities flushed apparently "expelled a lot of mucous" and was quite unpleasant.

Mandawa Castle

Dinner that evening was in a restaurant on the top floor of the beautiful Mandawa Castle Hotel. It claims to "revive the whole idea of luxury in a royal yet contemporary elegance" and boasts that "family portraits, antique cannons and arms add to the charm of this family-run resort where tradition still runs strong." The front of the building is unusual in that only half of it has been restored while the other half has been left to decay. According to Puru, this was the result of a family feud between two brothers who each owned half of the castle. But once inside, I could see that the propaganda produced for the castle wasn't lying. The hotel exuded charm and elegance, with chandeliers hanging from the decorated ceilings and mosaics covering the walls.

The inner courtyard of the castle surrounded a huge two-level pool beautifully illuminated under the dark skies.

The terrace had an outdoor dining area with local dancers resplendent in traditional costumes. A pavilion was lit up with candles, providing the perfect spot for romantic photos, and our group filled the air with laughter and cries of "My camera is the one on the left," and "It has an automatic flash, just hold the button down."

We completed our tour of the castle, admiring the portraits of the family and their ancestors, before heading upstairs to the restaurant. A buffet was laid out with home-made pickles and numerous hot and cold dishes, some of which were vegan. It was all really delicious. Linus and I had fun playing with our food as we tried to dine the traditional way without cutlery. Eating colourful curries with my fingers might not have been the wisest choice I've ever made when wearing a white top, but on this occasion I made it through the evening unstained.

As the meal drew to a close the head waiter came round with a journal, asking for comments from our tables. Shannon went first and wrote a fabulously verbose piece, a portion of which I'll share with you. "We loved the dessert. The halva was rich and divine. I really thought the soufflé was made of oranges - so light and heavenly... This hotel is a palace and the food and service is befitting of it." Not wishing to be outdone, our table handed the pen to Linus and looked at him hopefully. We were not disappointed. Highlights of his ramblings were "The rich variety of food made our table rapturous. Delight was found in the pickles and chutneys... We were particularly taken with the aesthetics - the frescoes are quite sublime." He handed the book to the third and final table, grinning widely. They accepted the challenge and applauded the eggplant dish, the service and atmosphere. "An authentic Indian experience which we will recommend to all our family and friends." And then it was back to the resort for a quick game of ping pong before bed.

Bikaner

We woke early in the morning, setting off before sunrise as we had a long day ahead of us. The journey from Mandawa to Bikaner takes about five hours, driving out into the desert. Madhukar stopped the coach briefly so we could photograph one of the many sunrises we saw during this tour of Rajasthan.

The Rat Temple

We took a slight detour around a truck lying across the main road to Bikaner, the front wheels obviously broken beyond repair as it lay in the dust, taking us past large houses surrounded by fields and through villages with the cleanest well-maintained homes and shops I'd seen so far. Painted in bright, fresh colours, they looked much newer than the havelis in Mandawa. We were on our way to the village of Deshnok and the highlight of our tour for some people – the Karni Mata Temple, also known as the Rat Temple. According to legend, the Goddess Karni Mata, a member of Charin clan, remained young and beautiful throughout her 150 years as a human. After her death, she became a rat. I don't know why she did that, but that's goddesses for you. They do strange things.

Followers of the Charin religion believe that when they die they will also be reincarnated as rats and that the ones in the temple are their ancestors. As for the rats, when they die they come back as humans. It's said that when Rajasthan was struck down by a plague the village of Deshnok was spared, protected by the holy rats. There are some 20,000 rats living within the temple, which is animal-proofed not to stop the rats from getting out but to stop predators from getting in. They're served food and milk daily and visitors can buy treats from stalls outside the temple. I thought at first that the beautifully packaged treats were for tourists to buy and eat, but many people buy them to share with the rats. It's considered lucky to eat something which has been nibbled on by a holy rat but it wasn't something I fancied doing.

We left our shoes at the drop-off point (yes, we had to wander around the rat-filled temple in our bare feet) and traversed the courtyard to enter through the beautiful carved doorway, guarded by marble lions lying on plinths. The inner courtyard had netting hanging above to stop birds from entering and annoying the rats, but I didn't spend much time looking up at it. I was too busy looking at my feet to make sure I didn't stand on anything either unpleasant or furry. Anyone who accidentally steps on a rat has to buy a solid silver rat statue and place it in the temple to atone for their sin.

I'd expected the floor to be covered in rat droppings but on this front I was pleasantly surprised. I'm not saying the floor was clean, but it seemed to be relatively poop-free. Rats scurried around this courtyard, pausing to drink from large bowls of milk put out for them.

I joined the line to enter the temple itself and slowly shuffled forward. The floor inside was covered in black and white tiles, which made it easy to spot rats running in front of me. It's supposed to be lucky if a rat runs over your feet, but I wasn't that fortunate and to be honest I wasn't too sad about it. The rats mostly stayed at the edges of the temple, sitting on platforms or peeking out of niches in the walls. Some sat on a large pile of corn husks while others hung from statues. They were all black or dark brown, with no sight of the fabled ultra-lucky white rat. Despite the vast amounts of food and the safe surroundings they all looked small, dirty and scraggy, unlike the big, glossy specimens some people keep as pets back home.

When I'd had my fill of the rats I wandered back outside and went to collect my shoes. As I was putting them on two ladies approached me shyly. "Can I?" said one hesitantly, pointing at my arm. I nodded and held it out for her to see. She and her friend gasped in amazement, rubbed the tattoo and then looked at their hands. They looked back at me with their eyes wide. "Not henna," said one. I shook my head. She mimed washing her arm to remove paint. Again I shook my head. She gave me the most beautiful smile and nodded her understanding. "Namaste," she said, blessing me as she led her friend away.

I met Chitranjan while waiting for the rest of the group to emerge from the temple, who showed me the treats he'd bought to take home for his family. He'd also bought a small wind-up rat which, from the look on his face, he intended to have a lot of fun with. He put it on the ground to demonstrate how well it moved and narrowly snatched it out of the way before a feral dog ate it. Linus also bought one of the toy rats and has had lots of fun with it back in Australia. He said if ever he goes back to the rat temple he'll be buying more of them.

Before we left Deshnok it seemed prudent to visit the bathroom because I didn't know how much travelling we had to do before our next stop. As I stood waiting my turn I confided in Lily that I'd never used a squat toilet before and was a little unsure of the correct method. To everyone's amusement, Lily then proceeded to give a fully-clothed demonstration as she talked me through various options for positioning oneself and one's clothing for a successful experience. Others joined in with words of advice such as "Don't squat too low or you won't be able to get back up," and "Make sure it doesn't go sideways," and "If you don't squat low enough it will all splash back up on you." I'm still laughing as I type this. Good words of advice indeed. I'm pleased to say that I achieved my objective without incident, although Shannon was not as lucky. "I peed on my shoe," she announced as we exited the building. Outside the men stood together laughing raucously. "We could hear everything that was said when you were in the bathroom," they chortled. "Lily, can you show us how to squat too?"

Junagarh Fort

After lunch in a restaurant near a murky lake (Lucinda and Linus had the vegetarian tandoori platter, of course) we spent some time at the Junagarh Fort under the care of a local guide. The original stone fort was built in 1478 by Rao Bika, the founder of Bikaner, but it wasn't until 1589 that Raja Rai Singhji, the sixth ruler of Bikaner, began construction of the fort which exists today. The Karan Palace within the fort was built in the 1930's by Karan Singh, with more floors added by his successors. In the 1960's Anup Singh added new palaces and special areas just for women. The Weather Palace and Ganga Niwas Palace were constructed in the 1800's. As a result of the ongoing construction the fort complex contains a mixture of architectural styles and some beautiful ornamentation. Over the years it's been attacked many times, but except for a one-day occupation by Kamran Mirza in 1534 it has never been captured.

As we walked from palace to palace I was surprised by how beautiful each one was. They were all covered in mosaics which were well preserved, clean and sparkly. Photos really don't capture how lovely they were.

The Public Audience Hall, built in the 1930's and decorated by Surat Singh in the late 1700's was particularly splendid, ornamented with hundreds of glass tiles.

It took a couple of hours to get around the fort, by which time I had little interest in seeing the objects displayed in the museum. For some reason Alan took a photo of a soup spoon in a glass case, which I had to ask him about later. Apparently it was of particular interest to him as a man with facial hair. The spoon had a specially designed cover which stopped the Maharaja's large moustache from getting dirty when he ate soup. Sadly the photo of the spoon in its dirty glass case was blurred, so you'll just have to use your imagination.

An ongoing problem I had with the forts of Rajasthan was that they were all huge, and there was just too much to take in. So many palaces to keep track of. So many lattice-covered windows through which I could peek at the world outside. So many mirrored ceilings, carvings of deities and tiled mosaics. I'd recommend a visit to all of the ones we went to, but I'd recommend getting an audio guide that you can turn on and off at will while setting your own pace. Our local guides were all nice people, but it always took hours and hours to get around the sites as we stood around listening to them talk. And talk. Even the expert listeners in the group faded out after the first hour or so. By the time we left Junagarh Fort even Puru expressed amazement at how long it had taken us. "I think you are the slowest group I've ever had," he said, shaking his head sadly.

A Blast From the Past

It was late afternoon by the time we left the fort and we were all tired after our early start, long drive and guided tours. We arrived at the Karni Bhawan Hotel, situated out of town and surrounded by grass. We were given the standard greeting received in most of the hotels of a garland around our necks and a blob of paint on our foreheads before Alan and I were shown to our room. After climbing three flights of stairs we emerged on the rooftop, across which we trudged to our suite, disturbing pigeons as we went. We were in an isolated unit secured by padlocked doors which when opened revealed a blast from the past.

I don't think anything had been changed in the room since the 1930's and it was like stepping back in time into the art deco period. The bed was big, the shower had warmer water than others I'd used in the recent past, and the pigeons outside the window cooed charmingly. But the best thing about the room was its location - the view of the sun setting over Bikaner from our private rooftop patio was spectacular.

Feasting at a Farmhouse

Later that evening we journeyed out into the countryside, speeding down dark roads and swerving in and out of our lane, eliciting shrieks from halfway down the coach as we pulled into the headlights of oncoming traffic again and again. After a while Puru asked Madhukar to slow down a little as he didn't want anyone in his group to have a heart attack. I'm fairly sure we weren't ever in real danger, but even I had been a little alarmed by some of the apparent near-misses with other vehicles. We'd been travelling for about an hour when our driver turned into a very narrow laneway and squeezed the coach through overgrown hedges and into a parking lot.

Dinner was a buffet affair served in the grassy courtyard of a farmhouse. A huge bonfire burned brightly under the black sky, dimly illuminating musicians playing under a tree. After a beer or two Alan needed the bathroom and headed over to the farmhouse. "Use the tree over there," the farmer instructed him, pointing the way. Alan did as told, then checked with the other men that they had been given the same instructions. He was quite relieved when they confirmed that the tree was indeed the place to go and that he hadn't taken what was intended to be a joke literally. We passed the evening eating, drinking and dancing under the stars before dozing our way back to the hotel.

Jaisalmer

The next day we travelled through the desert to Jaisalmer, a trading centre for the nomadic people of the area, and we had to travel a long way to get there. Bikaner was left behind in a cloud of dust as we drove along, stopping after a few hours for a drink at a roadside café. When we departed we took a slight detour by driving up the wrong side of a divided highway until we found a gap in the partition between the lanes, then drove the rest of the way to Jaisalmer on the correct side of the road, much to everyone's relief. This wasn't an unusual act in Rajasthan. The government built a number of toll roads with two lanes on either side of a concrete meridian. The gaps in the partition are few and far between, so it's acceptable to drive up the wrong side of the highway in order to access shops and cafes dotted along the side of the road. The same rule applied to roadworks, which could be avoided by driving through a gap in the meridian and into oncoming traffic.

We didn't stop again until Puru spotted something of interest in the desert plains. "This is a camel daycare," he informed us. The camels were owned by people in the neighbouring villages and were taken into the desert by the "daycare" manager, who returned them to their owners in the evening. He was very happy to pose for pictures (in exchange for cash, of course).

There were about 25 camels in the group, including a mother with her baby. They looked at us all impassively as we took photos, relieved to be out of the coach and able to stretch our legs. And then it was back on board for more driving across the desert, stopping only once at a railway crossing while we waiting for the train to pass.

After what seemed like an eternity we pulled into a café for lunch. To my delight, there was a mushroom curry on the menu. I hadn't seen any other mushroom dishes earlier in our trip, and I was very excited to be able to order one at last. It looked fabulous. Large chunks of mushrooms glimmering in a rich, thick sauce. I chased a mushroom around the bowl until it landed on my fork and I prepared to get a little taste of paradise. And then it happened. The mushroom saw its opportunity to escape and took a giant leap towards freedom. It landed on my pale green t-shirt and rolled down, leaving a thick trail of sauce behind it until landing in the folds of my skirt, where it hid quietly, hoping not to be seen. I was quite taken by surprise that my food would behave in such an unruly manner. The amount of mess created by one little mushroom was quite remarkable, and was way beyond the "blot it with a napkin and you'll be OK" stage. I sighed. Then, not to be defeated by a fungus, I tucked into the remaining mushrooms and enjoyed every morsel.

After lunch I retrieved my backpack from the coach and did a quick change in the washrooms. The attendant was very sympathetic, indicating that some of her saris had suffered similar indignities. I've since recreated the recipe, if not the entire messy experience, at home and have enjoyed it thoroughly. If you buy my book "HELP! There's a VEGAN Coming For Dinner - Indian Style" you can cook it too. But don't wear your best clothes when eating it.

About seven hours had passed since leaving Bikaner when we pulled up into the courtyard in front of the beautiful Mandir Palace Hotel, where we were greeted by a doorman displaying a moustache worthy of a place in Lily's collection of facial hair photos. We were served a vivid green drink, decorated with flowers, and daubed with paint before being shown to our rooms. I plopped down on the bed while Alan went to have a shower, laughing as I heard him talking to himself in a frustrated tone. When I went into the bathroom I realised what the problem was. The water from the shower flowed along the edge of the bathtub and onto the floor. It wasn't the first time in India we'd had to wade through puddles to get to the toilet, and I was fairly sure it wouldn't be the last.

Just as the sun was starting to go down, we met Puru in the lobby and were hurried onto the waiting coach. "Quickly!" he told Madhukar. "We don't want to be late!" Our appointment was to watch the sun set over the city of Jaisalmer, viewed from a hilltop with the tombs of long-dead people behind us. It was quite crowded on the hill, but as the sun sank below the horizon a hush descended as we watched the day draw to an end and night creep in.

A Warm Welcome from a Talkative Man

Dinner tonight was our first experience of eating in a family home, hosted by a man whom Lucinda refers to, perhaps with some justification, as "the most boring person in the world." Madhukar dropped us in Jaisalmer and we walked through the dark streets until we reached our destination. A cow stood outside of the home next door, mooing loudly. "She's come home for her dinner," Puru said. "Cows wander wherever they want, but they always come home when they're hungry."

I was hungry too. It had been a long day, and lunch was a distant memory. Our host greeted us at the door. "Welcome! Namaste! Come in! Come in!" He gave us a tour of his multi-roomed home, which he shared with his wife, his daughter, his son, his son's wife and their small child. His brother lived next door with his own wife, children and grandchildren. Both families usually ate together in the evenings, totalling about 16 people as far as I can work out.

Three women were at work in the kitchen, one stirring things on a stove while the younger ones sat on the floor chopping vegetables and making chapattis. "Please come in and sit down," said our host, gesturing towards one of the rooms. We placed ourselves on cushions on the floor and the lucky ones leaned back against a wall. The last ones to enter sat on the large bed which occupied most of the room. Our host took his seat in a plastic chair in the corner and began to talk. And talk. He told us he talks for a living, sitting for an entire day sharing his wisdom with his followers, pausing neither to eat nor drink nor to go to the bathroom. He talked to us about many things over the next two hours, although felt like much longer.

My concentration faded in and out (admittedly more out than in) but I caught snippets such as "A marriage is like a cart. If the wheels are not the same size the cart will fall over," and "Don't pay to go out for meals. Eat food in your own home. This is the better way." Hm. We were paying to go out and eat in his home. "Give away your gifts for free. Don't be greedy." In the room next door his daughter was applying henna to any ladies who wanted it, "for a free will donation." "Don't drink chai. For me it is the road to ruin." Apparently his wife didn't share his views on this, and she smiled indulgently while giving out cups of steaming milky chai to those who wanted it. I didn't enjoy his ramblings, but I did enjoy dinner. It was a vegetarian thali with curried potatoes, spiced cabbage, tomatoes with cumin, rice with vegetables and deep-fried puffs of bread. I didn't eat the home-made yoghurt, but not because our host was expounding the virtues of a non-dairy diet while his wife and daughter-in-law served the food. He talked about many, many things, but I'm afraid I can't share all his wisdom with you. Perhaps you should go to Jaisalmer, sit at his feet for eight hours or so and pray you don't need to pee.

Jaisalmer Fort

After a great buffet breakfast, including sweet mini bananas and a curry or two, it was time for a visit to Jaisalmer Fort, one of the largest fortifications in the world. It was built in 1156 by Rawal Jaiswal and strengthened in 1276 by King Jetsi while resisting an invasion by the Sultan of Delhi.

The fort has three layers of walls. The outermost wall is made up of stone blocks which are used to reinforce the hill on which it is built. The middle wall surrounds the outer edges of the fort while the inner wall was used to drop boiling oil and water on enemies as they tried to enter the city. Around 3-4,000 people currently live inside the fortified city.

We stood in the square before our climb up the hill, looking at the yellow sandstone building shining in the sun.

Cows milled around among the motorcycles and tuk-tuks. Beth stepped back to keep out of the way of an angry-looking bull and stepped in some dung. I was surprised that nobody else had done this so far, as there were numerous manure deposits on the streets of Jaisalmer. Our guide for the day took her to a faucet to wash off the poo while a young girl demonstrated her rope-walking skills to anyone who would watch. "She should be in school," said Puru, shaking his head at the girl's mother.

We climbed up the cobbled road and entered the fort, passing through four massive gates as we zigzagged upwards until entering the fortified city through a gateway guarded by two large statues of elephants. We pushed our way along the busy streets until we arrived at the Jain Temple.

Leaving our shoes outside the temple under the watchful eye of a professional shoe-guard, we entered through a large carved wooden door. Inside were carvings as far as the eye could see. Every pillar, every wall and every section of the ceiling was carved with images of deities or ornate patterns. It was beautiful in a cold, austere sort of way.

Gates covered the front of alcoves in which sat statues of people sitting in the lotus position, silver dots on their chests and shoulders, surrounded by carvings of elephants and women. "You've got to go and see that pillar over there," someone whispered to me, pointing the way. I went to have a look, and found a carving of a man with a very impressively sized reproductive organ. Yes, I took a photo. No, I'm not sharing it with you - you'll have to go and have a look for yourself.

We exited the temple and continued our tour of the city, admiring the havelis as we passed by, some of which were hundreds of years old with beautiful sandstone carvings. Our tour took us through the central square, in which there was a smooth stone water spout which was used by residents before the development of indoor plumbing.

Obviously having access to running water inside

buildings is a good thing, but the water-management system of Jaisalmer Fort wasn't designed with this in mind. Water drainage has become a major problem, with seepage into the clay soil under the fort causing some buildings to collapse. Conservation agencies are working together to stabilize the city.

Not far from the water spout we climbed some steep, worn, uneven steps to the top of the fortress walls from where we could see Jaisalmer spread out before us.

After climbing down the steps back to the main street, treading carefully so that we didn't slip and fall onto the people ahead of us, we wandered along the narrow streets, passing bookstores selling textbooks in many languages and computer stores offering to put our photos onto a disc or two.

Outside a café serving "the best Italian cappuccino in Jaisalmer" were stalls selling carved wood printing blocks. Men and women sold fruits and vegetables from cloths laid out the floor.

Samosas were being deep-fried in huge oil-filled woks outside cafes. Of all the forts we'd seen on our tour Jaisalmer was my favourite by far. This was a living fort, full of the sights and smells I'd expected to find in India. Following our guide through the streets of the fortified city was a very different experience to Old Delhi, where it was almost impossible to move. In Jaisalmer the narrow streets were busy but not packed, and people could move out of the way of motorcycles as they drove along slowly. Everything seemed brighter and cleaner in Jaisalmer than it had in Delhi. The air was fresher and even the cows looked fatter and healthier.

We stopped for a tour of an ornately carved haveli which dated back to 1885. Two stone elephants stood by the doorway, indicating that this was the home of someone important. A sparrow had made a nest in one of the niches above the doorframe and sat looking down on us as we entered.

We were invited to climb the stairs to see the beautiful ceiling in the upper rooms, which also happened to be a huge showroom for local crafts. "This is made from real camel bone," a salesman said, trying to press a carved box into my hands. "Lovely to store pretty jewels inside." I didn't take it from him and shook my head. "No thanks. It's very nice but not something I need." The boxes, he told me, were made out of camels which died naturally in the desert and were then harvested for their skin and bones. I assume these camels belonged to someone as Puru had said there were no wild camels left in Rajasthan, only those owned by traders or families. But regardless of the camels' natural deaths, I had no desire to put carved bones into my backpack and give them to friends back home.

Our friendly guide handed his followers back to Puru, who led us down lanes to K.B Cooperative Arts where we could see (and, of course, purchase) locally made fabric goods. Our group sat on benches around the edges of a showroom and watched while the salesman unfurled bedspread after bedspread to show us the designs. When the attention of the group noticeably faded he invited Lily to try on an ornate red and gold wedding dress with veil, covered in sequins. Linus stood next to her, squeezed into a flamboyant sequined jacket at least two sizes too small for him. It was Alan's turn next, called up to model a brightly coloured turban which the salesman weaved expertly around his head. Ali Baba's look was finally complete.

Alan and I snuck away from the bedspread and tablecloth showroom and asked if we could have a quiet look at some shawls. We had a list of people we wanted to buy gifts for, and shawls from a Jaisalmer arts cooperative would be perfect for some of them. The store owner gave us a brief talk about the types of shawls on each shelf and then left us to look through them. It was really nice to be able to shop without any pressure to buy anything, and we took our time choosing the ones we wanted.

When the owner returned he said "I'll give you a discount because you've bought more than three. Come this way to pay." Despite the discount I don't think he was really doing us a big favour - we could have paid the same price for shawls in Canada - but we knew the gifts would be appreciated back home. He ran Alan's credit card through an old fashioned machine while we sat and drank tea, chatting about places we'd visited. The owner's English was very good, which he said was a result of talking to tourists. He put our purchases into bags made from recycled saris and offered more tea while we waited for the others in the group to join us. Puru appeared and suggested getting a tuk-tuk for us if we wanted to go back to the hotel. We had some shopping enthusiasts in the group and they might be there for quite a while yet. Linus and Lucinda had also had enough for the day, so we squeezed into a tuk-tuk and went back to the hotel to relax for a short while before returning to the city for dinner.

Some of the ladies elected to try on saris provided by local families. I've never been one to play dress-up and was comfortable and happy in my travel wear. We sat on cushions around the low tables of a rooftop restaurant watching the sun set over the city, and it was quite beautiful. Of all the places I visited in India, the "living fort" of Jaisalmer was my favourite.

Camel Safari

We had some time in the morning to relax by the pool with our books or do some shopping in the hotel store. I'd had a look the day before and really liked some of the table runners, much more than I liked the ones in the cooperative arts shop in Jaisalmer. I selected two small ones which I knew I had spots for back home then tried to get the attention of the salesman. He was under Lily's spell as she acted out going for a camel ride in the desert. She did a good job of it, I have to say. The salesman invited her to go for a ride on his motorcycle, which Lily declined. "I have to go now. My friends are waiting for me." The salesman reluctantly let her leave and sauntered over to see what the boring middle-aged woman wanted, cheering up dramatically when he saw that I wanted to buy something. He told me prices were not negotiable, but I'd heard him telling Lily he would give her a reduced price if she bought more than one item. I held my ground and got some money off the "special prices for tourists", marvelling at how expensive India was turning out to be.

We spent the afternoon sitting in the coach, driving down a bumpy road which went on for miles out into the desert plains. We were short by one person, leaving Shannon behind in the hotel to rest until we returned to retrieve her the following day. She'd caught the cough some days before and now had bronchitis, for which she was taking an assortment of Indian medicines. It was very disappointing for her to have to miss the camel safari but taking bronchitis out into the dessert wouldn't have been much fun.

There wasn't much to see as we drove into the wilderness except sand and the occasional wind turbine or small family compound, complete with mud walls and straw-thatched houses.

As we drove past a large military base Puru informed us that we were close to the border with Pakistan. "Don't let your camel run away with you or you will end up over the border and we'll have to leave you behind!" he laughed. I'm fairly sure he was joking.

Not long after that we pulled up outside our home for the night, located in the middle of nowhere. It was odd to see a "holiday resort" sitting in an isolated patch of desert, surrounded by nothing but sand and an occasional tree or two. We walked through the mud and stone reception building and exited into a sand courtyard. Chairs were arranged round an arena ready for our evening entertainment. Nearby, steps led down to a sunken, tiled swimming pool, which obviously hadn't had any water in it for quite some time.

Our accommodation could be seen across an expanse of sand, and after receiving the traditional greeting and a cool drink Alan and I wandered off to see our home for the night, aware of military jets flying overhead from time to time, shattering the peace.

The stained canvas tent was hotter than hell inside despite Puru's repeated warnings that it would be cold in the desert. He was wearing a fleece over his t-shirt and had donned a thick hat to keep his head warm despite the air temperature being a very pleasant 25'C (77'F), which Puru insisted was cold. Inside the tent was much hotter than outside and I was grateful to see a fan next to the hard wooden beds.

Alan sat on the bed closest to him, which cracked ominously. "I really need to pee," he said uncomfortably. "Did you see a toilet anywhere?" I shook my head. "I didn't see a building marked toilets." He picked up a pail sitting by the table. "Do you think we're supposed to use this?" I looked at the proffered object and shrugged. This was India. We'd seen people squatting by railway tracks and urinating openly by the side of the road. Alan had peed against a tree at a farmhouse. At this point using a bucket seemed like something he should consider. "I'll take it out behind the tent," he said, grabbing the bucket and opened the rear flap to step outside. He stopped and gasped. "Take a look at this!" I rolled off my bed and went to see what the excitement was about. Attached to our canvas tent was a tiled bathroom with a western style toilet, hosepipe shower and a small sink. We looked at each other in amazement, then Alan handed me the bucket. "I think this is a garbage can," he said, grinning.

A Sunset Camel Ride

Late in the afternoon I met up with the rest of the group in the campsite parking lot. Camels were sitting around waiting for us, chewing thoughtfully. Brightly coloured fabric covered the saddles and their reins were decorated with coloured stones and ribbons. It wasn't until I looked at the photos later that I realised the camels had a large spike through their noses, which was attached to the reins. I'd assumed their handlers used bits in the mouth similar to the ones used by horses and I wasn't happy to see the spikes. It must be quite painful.

Puru climbed onto the closest camel and demonstrated how to stay on while the camel stood up and, perhaps more importantly, how to not fall off when it sat down again. "Lean well back!" he instructed us. "Or you will fall off over the camel's head." I've experienced falling off horses and had been quite badly damaged the one time I was projected over a horse's head, so this was obviously something I wanted to avoid doing in the middle of a desert. I looked at the camels wondering which one to pick when a wizened old man approached me. He pointed to his camel and waved me to approach. The camel turned his head looked at me impassively as I put my foot in the stirrup and plopped onto the front seat of the saddle. His handler clicked at the camel, who proceeded to stand up while I prayed that I wouldn't fall off. When everyone was uncomfortably seated we were led off into the desert plains to see the sunset.

We travelled slowly for about half an hour before stopping and clumsily dismounting, leaving our camels and their owners sitting in the sand while we climbed a high dune to get a better view. There was still time before the sunset so Puru challenged us to a race up a sand dune. He ran down the dune and waited at the bottom for his competitors to arrive. Puru was determined to uphold the honour of India and vowed he would win at all costs. Ryan ran down to represent Northern Ireland and Alan joined him as the token Canadian. Lily raced down to uphold England's honour while Angie and

Linus doubled Australia's chance of a win. New Zealand was left without hope - the Aunties were past the age of wanting to run up sand dunes and Shannon was back in Jaisalmer. My money was on the local boy because I'd seen him sneakily slip off his shoes to make it easier to run in the sand. The countdown began. "GO!" and they were off. India got off to a flying start but was quickly overtaken by Northern Ireland, with Canada, England and Australia in hot pursuit. Had I placed money on the local boy I would have gone home poorer, but Puru graciously accepted defeat and went back down the dune to retrieve his shoes.

We sat in the sand, carefully avoiding the huge dung beetles scurrying around, and watched brightly dressed ladies, who seemingly appeared out of nowhere, dance while we waited for the sun to sink behind the horizon. It was quite magical.

Once the sun had set, I wandered back down to where my camel was waiting and climbed on as elegantly as possible. The handler effortlessly swung himself up behind me and clicked for his camel to stand up. We set off at a slow pace and were soon at the back of the pack. "He like to run," came a voice from behind me. I wasn't quite sure how to take that, but it would become clear later on what he meant. I watched as my tour group got smaller in the distance and wondered if I should be concerned. The German tour group from Mandawa, which I'd spotted on the dunes some time before, overtook my plodding camel. As they became dots in the distance a voice behind me asked "You ready?"

Certain that I didn't have much choice in the matter, I gave my assent. He flipped the reins once and the camel shot forward like a speeding bullet. Boy, did this camel like to run! We hurtled forwards, me gripping the saddle until my knuckles went white. I squeezed as tightly as I could with my legs but was unable to stop myself from going bump, bump, bump as I bounced along. Flash, as I thereafter called the camel, quickly caught up with the Germans and overtook them one by one, leaving them behind in a cloud of dust. He shot past the slower ones from my group before screeching to a halt back at the campsite. It was quite a ride and I'm sure Flash gave me a smug look as I climbed off, my legs shaking slightly. Flash's handler gave me a nod as I handed him a tip. "He like to run fast," he said, patting his camel. I smiled and nodded, thanking them both before asking my wobbly legs to carry me back to the tent.

A shower before dinner would have been nice, but Puru had told us that there would only be hot water between 6 and 6:30 the following morning. "What time will we be leaving?" I asked. "Six fifteen."

The dinner buffet was served in the main courtyard,

where we sat in chairs around the central entertainment area, eating food from the buffet and drinking lager. We ate pakoras and chewed on spiced desert beans while a transgendered person entertained us with dancing and gave an impressive performance while balancing objects on her head. (Interesting fact: "transgender" became a legal third gender in India, alongside "male" and "female", in 2014).

The German tour group boarded their coaches for the long, dark drive across the desert back to their hotel in Jaisalmer while my fellow travellers and I retired to our hot tents, passing a sleepless night sweating on our hard beds in the Rajasthan desert. It was fabulous.

Jodhpur

I rose long before the sun did and took a cold shower sitting on a plastic stool, contemplating the fuzzy feeling which had developed in my head overnight and the pain in my throat. "I think I might have caught the bug," I told Alan sadly. He was still feeling fine and made encouraging noises about me being able to nap on the coach on the way to Jodhpur some six hours away. As we grabbed a quick breakfast I bemoaned the fact that my emergency medical supplies didn't include cold and flu treatments, which I strongly suspected I would be in need of before the end of the day. But it was impossible to feel sorry for myself for long, knowing that having a flu bug while seeing the sights of India was infinitely more exciting than being back home in Canada. I boarded the coach, settled back in my seat and watched the sun rise over the desert.

The journey passed without major incident as we drove out of the desert plains and through tiny villages, swerving from time to time around cows standing in the middle of the road. We took yet another detour off the main highway to avoid a broken-down truck blocking the road, bumping our way down a small cracked side-road until we could access the main one again.

After a brief stop to retrieve Shannon from Jaisalmer we continued our journey to Jodhpur. She looked much better than before, although she was still coughing. I suspected that it wouldn't be long before I joined in with the coughing-chorus on the coach and closed my eyes trying to sleep it off.

Mehrangarh Fort

Our first tour of the day took place at the Mehrangarh Fort in the center of Jodhpur. Construction of the fortress was started in 1459 by the founder of Jodhpur, Rao Jodha. Most of the fort, however, was built in the 1600's by Jaswant Singh of Marwar. It's been preserved as a museum containing many artifacts, and it usually takes people two to three hours to make their way around. We were supplied with audio guides and set free to wander. I tried to listen to the guide but my head was pounding and the last thing I wanted was someone talking constantly in my ear as I dragged myself around the fort. Alan found the audio guide to be quite interesting and filled me in with facts and figures as we wandered around.

For those who enjoy museums, the Mehrangarh Fort is one not to be missed. There's a fabulous view of the Blue City from the upper ramparts, from where the Umaid Bhawan Palace can also be seen. There are many carvings showing the lives and culture of the Royal Family. There's a display of cannons and some walls have the imprints from cannon balls fired in years gone by. The fort museum has also has a large display of costumes, palanquins and Howdahs (elephant seats) that were used during battles.

I let Alan wander around much of the fort alone, taking as long as he wanted, while I sat down on seats dotted around the courtyards and watched the world go by. As I waited on a small bench outside one of the buildings an American lady plopped down next to me. “It’s hot, isn’t it?” she gushed, flapping a tourist information sheet in front of her face. I smiled my agreement, thinking of Puru walking around in his body warmer and tweed hat.

She was about to say something else when a young man squeezed onto the bench between us. “Take it now,” he instructed his friend, who placed himself in front of us, camera at the ready. “What are you doing? Go away!” insisted the woman, giving the young man a bit of a push. I leaned forward and spoke past him. “It’s much faster if you just smile for the camera, honestly. Doesn’t this happen to you all the time?” Apparently this was the first time she’d encountered such behaviour, having only arrived in India the day before. “If I smile for your friend will you go away?” she asked our unwanted companion. “Yes. Of course.” We turned towards the camera and gave our best forced smiles while the young man gave a big thumbs up. “Thank you so much, beautiful ladies,” he enthused as he left. The American woman looked at me in horror. “Does that happen often?” “All the time,” I replied, much to her dismay. All. The. Time.

We stopped for lunch in the castle café, and it was a relief to sit in the shade with a glass of cold soda water with lime. Back in Delhi Puru had recommended this drink to everyone to help combat the effects of too much spice, but I drank it simply because it was refreshing on a hot day. It came either sweet, salty or both sweet and salty, which I had once and thought was revolting. I had a soothing bowl of red lentil soup for lunch with vegetable pakoras, served with the standard Rajasthan dip – tomato ketchup.

By the time we reached the exit I was struggling to keep going. My temperature had rocketed, my head was ready to explode and I’d developed a very impressive cough.

Alan found Puru and told him I wasn't well. Instead of dragging me on the planned walk around Jodhpur he bundled me into a tuk-tuk which took me through the bustling market and back to the coach. Madhukar kindly turned on the air conditioning and I huddled up on the back seat coughing the afternoon away in peace and quiet while he and Chitranjan sat outside drinking chai and reading the newspaper.

Local Lassi

Later, Alan brought photos of Jodhpur for me to see what I'd missed. Their first stop had been at the Shri Mishriala Hotel, which is apparently the best place in Jodhpur to sample the yoghurt-based drink known as lassi. Their speciality was "Makhaniya Lassi", made from curds, saffron, cardamom and enough sugar to sink a battleship. "It was like diabetes in a glass," I was told.

Their next stop was the market, where handmade pots

were being painted by local artists. Other vendors had long rows of saris strewn on the floor for interested shoppers to look though.

Their walk back to the coach took them along streets dotted with the blue houses for which Jodhpur is famous. Traditionally blue homes were the residences of Brahmin, a Hindu caste of priests and teachers of the sacred texts, but in Jodhpur members of other castes also painted their houses blue. It's claimed that the colour wards off mosquitoes and keeps the interior cool.

Umaid Bhawan Palace

The final stop of the day was at the museum in the Umaid Bhawan Palace. I stayed in the coach and anticipated a detailed review of it when the others returned, but the best report I got was "It had some funky clocks in it." They saw some old cars, a large flag and lots of "old things in cases" but everyone was really tired and I don't think even the best museum in the world could have piqued their interest at this point.

Only a small portion of the palace is open to the public. Alongside the museum is a hotel with 70 luxurious suites decorated in art deco style, one of which has a bathtub carved from a single block of pink marble. The remainder of the huge building is home to Jodhpur's royal family, and is one of the largest private residences in the world.

With a collective sigh of relief we left the palace and headed off to our considerably more humble dwelling on the outskirts of Jodhpur.

We spent the night at the beautiful, tranquil Mandore Guest House, sleeping in mudded huts surrounded by plants and statues. When we arrived the owner showed me immediately to my room while the others sat in the gardens for the official "welcome". He knocked on the door shortly afterwards bearing a pot of lemon and herb tea. "This will make you feel better," he sympathised. I settled down into one of the comfy chairs and sipped my hot tea, grateful for both the tea and his thoughtfulness.

The next day Puru organised a trip to a chemist for a "drug run". I resisted the pharmacist's attempts to sell me antibiotics and came away with flu capsules, cough liquid and throat lozenges. I asked Puru if I should take the flu capsules every four hours and he looked at me in horror. Once every 12 hours would be enough, he assured me. I don't know what was in the drugs but they did a good job of reducing most of the flu symptoms, even if they made me feel a bit "high." The cough, however, continued for weeks after I returned home and was something I could have happily lived without.

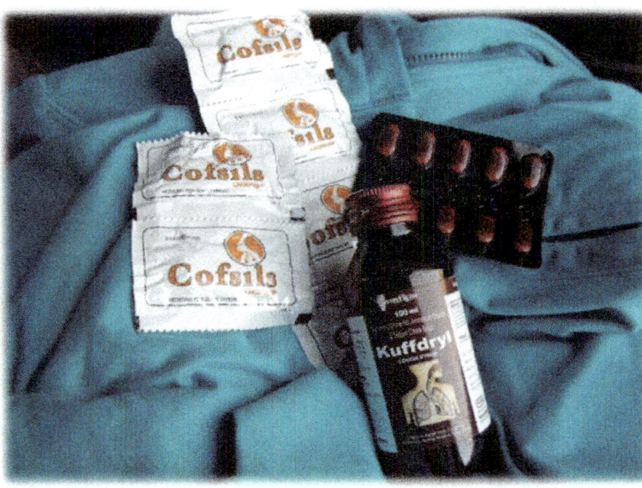

Udaipur

After an early breakfast of rice and lentils we set off on the final leg of our Rajasthan coach trip, embarking on a five hour drive from Jodhpur to Udaipur. We were making a day of it by stopping at a couple of places on the way and wouldn't get to "the most romantic spot in India" until early evening. I didn't mind having a day of sitting on a coach ahead of me given that I was dosed up on flu medications and just wanted to chill out for a while.

Pukhraj Durry Udhyog

We'd been driving for about half an hour when Alan nudged me and showed me a compass on his iPad. "I don't know where we're going, but Udaipur is in the other direction." It transpired that we were making a stop at the Salawas village weaving cooperative Pukhraj Durry Udhyog to see hand-made durries. Our coach slowly reversed into the driveway and we were invited by the owner to take off our shoes and enter the enclosure where his family made their rugs. There are about forty-eight families in the village working in their own homes and selling their creations through the cooperative store.

Chhotaram Prajapat talked at length about famous visitors to the cooperative such as Prince Charles, to whom they had gifted samples of their work, while he and his wife demonstrated how the durries were made on an old loom. We were served drinks and shown many, many durries made from cotton or silk yarn, goat or camel hair, jute or wool.

There was no pressure to buy and I was happy to sit in the shade drinking strong black coffee while others chose durries and arranged to have them shipped back home. Alan appeared at my side. "You have to go to the toilet in the building across that field," he pointed the way, "and take your camera." I was intrigued, so I retrieved my shoes and went to investigate. The small mud building contained a toilet designed to make both foreigners and Indians happy. There was a seat for those who preferred to sit but there were extensions on the side for the feet of those who would rather squat. Brilliant!

Ranakur Jain Temple

After stopping for lunch at a restaurant with lush green gardens we finally made it to the main highlight of the day - the Jain Temple at Ranakur. According to legends, this spectacular place was built in the 15th century by a local Jain businessman called Dharma Shah. He had a vision of a celestial plane and he decided to build a temple resembling what he saw. Despite interviewing many artists and sculptors, he wasn't happy with any of their designs until he met a sculptor named Depak. King Rana Kumbha gave land to Dharanashah to build both the temple to honour Adinath, the founder of the Jain religion, and to build a village nearby. The village was abandoned shortly after being built and became completely overgrown by the jungle but was later reclaimed and reinhabited. It's not usually visited by tourists despite its proximity to the Ranakur temple.

Before entering the temple, we had to remove our shoes and leave behind any leather objects such as handbags or belts. Women had to make sure our legs were covered to well below the knee. Taking a camera into the temple required a "donation" of a set amount for each camera, with an extra "donation" for cell phones capable of taking photos. This was monitored by a guard with a metal detector making sure there was one ticket for each item. There were also guards inside the building deterring tourists from photographing statues of deities. We were warned that receiving a blessing from a Jain monk would be followed by an aggressive request for a donation, which was verified by some of our group as we reconvened after the tour.

Carved white marble pillars stretched as far as the eye could see, supporting intricately sculpted balconies and a domed ceiling. The building contains about 29 halls and 1444 pillars, no two of which are the same. I wandered around in silence, stopping at specific places to listen to my audio guide until I tired of having someone drone on in my ear about the history of Jainism. The temple, it has to be said, was awesome and the best by far of all the temples we visited in Rajasthan. Statues of Buddha with their eyes painted open gazed back at tourists peeking into their shrines. Snakes intertwined in intricate patterns. It really was beautiful.

As I passed by a tree growing in the middle of a courtyard I encountered a small boy laying on the floor having a loud tantrum, ignoring the sign hanging on a pillar above his head requesting silence in the temple. His mother looked at me and smiled. I smiled back. My own kids were tantrum experts when they were young and I'd done my share of waiting patiently in public places while they loudly expressed themselves. We both looked down at her son and laughed. I saw her again a bit later being scolded by a security guard after her son crawled underneath a lucky elephant's belly once too often and was now sitting under the statue refusing to budge.

After spending a considerable amount of time in the temple it was time to continue our journey to Udaipur, stopping briefly to photograph monkeys through the coach windows. "Can't we get out?" Shannon asked. Puru shook his head. "They would attack you looking for food. Monkeys here will bite you. It's better not to get too close."

It was dark when we eventually reached Udaipur. Here we bade a fond farewell to our coach driver Madhukar and the ever helpful Chitranjan before climbing into the waiting taxis which would take us to the Lake Pichola Hotel. Our room was very nice, but the best part was the balcony overlooking the lake. We had dinner in the rooftop restaurant, watching the city lights shimmer on the water while eating curries and drinking lager. Happy days indeed.

Octopussy

The following morning we walked along the streets of Udaipur, following in the footsteps of Ian Fleming's James Bond in the movie Octopussy. After returning home Alan and I settled down to watch Octopussy to see if we recognised any of the places Bond saw. As he raced by the steps at the bottom of the Jain Temple we pointed and exclaimed "We were there! Right there!" while thinking it looked a lot cleaner and quieter in the movie than it did in real life. As we passed an art shop

Puru told us to make a note of where it was as it would help guide us back to the hotel at the end of the day. This was one of the few opportunities when we could wander around on our own in the afternoon. But first we had to visit the Hindu Temple in the middle of town, followed by a guided tour around the City Palace.

The temple was a fraction of the size and splendour of the one we'd seen the day before in Rankapur but it was throbbing with people entering to worship or meditate in the main hall. The outside was covered in carvings of elephants, horses and deities similar to those seen at the other temples we'd visited.

From there we walked up to the grounds of the City Palace, which according to legend was built on the site where Maharana Udai Singh met a hermit who told him to build a palace on the hilltop. It was built in many different stages starting around 1559 and added to over the years by different Maharanas. It's one of the largest royal palaces in India.

Our guide for the day, like our guides at all the other forts and palaces we'd seen so far, was full of knowledge which he wished to impart, but even the most ardent listeners were getting restless by now. Puru had commented a few times that we were the slowest group he had ever escorted around Rajasthan and marvelled at the length of time it took us to get around the sites. But not this time. We marched from room to room, determined to make the most of the opportunity to have a free afternoon and not wishing to spend longer in the palace than we had to. Linus and Ryan took on the job of keeping our guide moving along at a rapid (for us) pace, and they did it remarkably well. There was time to admire the paintings, mirrored rooms, antiques and courtyards without spending an eternity in front of each treasure. I really wish we'd started doing this much, much earlier in the tour.

We met Puru at the Palace gate and he expressed surprise at the speed of our tour before taking us to a rooftop restaurant for lunch. A palm reader was on hand (pun intended) for those who wanted to make appointments to see him sometime during the afternoon. I declined the offer, as my previous encounter with a palm reader had been less than successful. He was the father of a friend and prided himself on his ability to read the future. He took my hand, studied it for quite some time then gave it back to me. "No." he said. "No?

What do you mean?" He shook his head. "Just no." And that was that. No palm reading for me. It didn't make me particularly inclined to pay someone to look at my palm in India, although the ones who had a reading said it was "interesting" and that they could relate to some of the things he said even though he wasn't 100 percent accurate. I think he was adept at reading people rather than palms, and find it hard to believe that our lives can be mapped according to lines in our skin.

We were finally free to wander, promising to meet Puru at five for a boat trip around the lake. Alan and I set off down the twisting alleys filled with stores selling silver, shoes, bags, leather goods and miniature paintings. We still needed to buy some gifts and selected a store full of painted papier-mâché boxes which would be fairly light to carry home. It was air conditioned inside so I was happy to let the store owner take his time showing us the different designs, shapes and sizes before making our selection.

Alan wanted to buy some t-shirts, so we opened negotiations at a market stall which was owned by a charming young man selling designs Alan liked. For the first time since arriving in India we haggled the price down to something we thought was reasonable and left happy. However, our happiness decreased significantly when the t-shirts shrank in the washing machine back home. Perhaps Alan should have washed them in a river like people do in Udaipur.

Despite the heat (and the noise (and the dirt)) it was quite pleasant walking around Udaipur and then sitting in a riverside café having a drink. I forgot that I shouldn't drink things with ice cubes in them and in a moment of weakness ordered iced tea. I looked at it for a while wondering what to do, thinking it would be rude to ask the server if the ice was made using tap water. "Why don't you just drink it through your lifestraw?" asked Alan. That was a good idea, allowing me to filter out any possible water-borne bugs while enjoying a cold drink.

The walk back to the hotel to meet Puru was quite amusing. Two drivers had tried to pass each other on a street only big enough for one vehicle at a time and had got stuck. Traffic was backed up in both directions and wouldn't be going anywhere until the two stuck cars were freed. We passed Shannon, who looked hot and frustrated in a stationary tuk-tuk after picking up some custom-made clothing from a local tailor. We arrived back at the hotel long before she did.

Sunset Cruising

Once everyone had made it back to the hotel, we boarded a boat from the hotel dock and spent half an hour cruising on the lake, watching the sun set behind the hills. Lake Pichola is artificial, dug in 1362 and filled with freshwater. It's one of several lakes created around Udaipur, maintained by dams and diverted rivers. We got a close-up view of the Lake Palace featured in Octopussy but didn't dock there. None of us were rich enough to step foot in the extremely expensive restaurant or stay in its luxurious rooms. Built of white marble in 1774, this palace has been visited by royalty from many countries and has been described as "the most romantic hotel in the world." I'll never have enough money to stay there, so I'll just have to take their word for it.

After returning to the hotel and grabbing a quick bite to eat, we met Puru in the lobby to go to a cultural show on the other side of the river. We set off later than he wanted and he marched us at quite a pace along the dark, uneven streets. Cars and tuk-tuks streamed by us. One got a little too close for comfort, nudging me into the open sewer at the side of the road where I tripped and fell over. Fortunately the worst damage done was to my pride, but I spent the first part of the show rubbing hand sanitizer into the scrapes on my knee rather than watching the performers. It stung, but I figured it was a wise thing to do under the circumstances. As I cleaned my wounds, ladies in decorative saris swirled on the stage doing traditional dances. A puppeteer made his puppets talk in squeaky voices while they re-enacted folk tales. But the highlight of the evening was an older woman who balanced pots on her head. I don't know why they didn't fall off, but she walked around confidently as they leaned over at a precarious angle.

Over drinks after the show Puru gave us bad news about our plans for the following day. The time of our flight back to Delhi had changed, so instead of spending the morning doing yoga and having a demonstration at the famous Spice Box cooking school we would be heading off to the airport instead. He promised to find something for us to do in Delhi to make up for it since we would be arriving earlier than originally planned. And he was true to his word.

New Delhi

We gathered in the hotel lobby after breakfast and waited for taxis to take us to the airport. And waited. And waited. Puru was showing signs of stress for the first time during the tour and disappeared a few times to make phone calls to find out where our transportation was. He was obviously relieved when the taxis turned up and he ushered us in four at a time while the drivers strapped random items of luggage to the roof. There was some concern that bags might get left behind, but everyone and everything arrived at the airport eventually.

We made it through the passport checks and waited in the airport lounge for our early flight. And waited. And waited. I have no idea what time we eventually boarded our delayed plane, but I kept myself amused by looking at the hundreds of photos on my camera while drinking tea and eating potato chips from the departure lounge shop. Alan picked up a local paper filled with adverts placed by men and women looking for a husband or wife. Some of them sounded quite attractive even though I didn't understand all the acronyms used. "Highly cultured exceptionally affluent royal family (Hindu) invites proposals for their exceptionally beautiful, very charming, smart, slim, well groomed, 1985 born (very young looking) 5'4" daughter." "HKG based w/well established business handsome modern Sindhi man 45 seeks alliance from suitable Sindhi girl."

The flight back to Delhi was uneventful, which is obviously the best kind of flight, and I grabbed my backpack before following Puru out to the taxis. There was a sign on the parking lot wall banning people from smoking, spitting, drinking alcohol and cooking. We don't get people cooking dinner in the airport parking lot in Ottawa, but maybe that's because it's covered in snow for half of the year?

The final night of the official tour was spent back at the Hotel Jivitesh, where we stayed when we first arrived in India. As we drove by the huge statue of Hanuman overlooking the highway it all seemed comfortably familiar. Our room this time was bigger and nicer than at the start of the tour, and I was ecstatic to find hot water coming out of the shower.

Home Cooked Delhi

We hadn't been there long before it was time to set out again, piling into the taxis taking us to Puru's promised event for the day - visiting a family in the suburbs on the other side of Delhi to have a home-cooked meal. Traffic was crazy as we slowly honked our way along the streets and it took us an hour or so to reach our destination. The taxis dropped us off in a clean, well maintained neighbourhood where we were met by our hostess for the evening. She walked us to her home and escorted us up the stairs to the third floor apartment she shared with her parents, grandmother, cousin, uncle and uncle's wife. Her sister had recently gotten married and had moved in with her husband's family.

She invited us to sit on the sofas and plastic chairs packed into the small living room, obviously happy to have us in her home. Grandma joined us for snacks before Uncle invited us to join him in the kitchen to watch him prepare dinner. It would have been a better if there had only been four of us, but we were a much bigger group than the space could hold. Some ended up on the balcony peeking in through the door and others watched from the living room while a lucky few stood on each other's toes in the kitchen itself.

It was fun to watch how "real" people actually cook dinner in Delhi. There are cookbooks on my shelf at home which insist that spices should be bought whole in very small quantities then roasted and ground just before using. I don't know about you, but I don't have time for that. I buy pre-ground spices and keep them in spice drawers ready for use. It seemed that Uncle shared my thoughts on this matter. He opened his spice tin, tipped some spices into a pan along with cauliflower and potatoes, gave it a stir then put the lid on. There was no fuss, no measuring and no grinding of freshly roasted spices. This was cooking I could relate to.

Rice was steaming away in a pressure cooker, which surprised me. I always cook it in an electric rice cooker which doesn't take up space on my stovetop. I hate pressure cookers; I like to be able to see what my food is doing while it's cooking and I can't do that if it's covered by a sealed lid. A pan of red lentils simmered on the stove next to a flat griddle onto which Uncle tossed chapattis.

After Uncle's cooking demonstration, our hostess invited us to join her sitting on a bed while she showed us photos of her sister's wedding. "Was it an arranged marriage?" someone asked. "Yes, of course. That's how we do it here," came the reply. She explained that her parents sometimes introduced her to potential husbands and she had the right to say yes or no. Sometimes she invited boys to meet her parents, and they could say yes or no. "It's very important that everyone is happy," she explained. "When a girl gets married she has to leave her own family and live with her husband's family, so it's good that everyone likes everyone else. I would never marry someone if my parents didn't like him and his family, and they would never make me marry someone if I didn't want to. Family is very important." We asked about dowries and were told that it's been illegal for many years to request a dowry. "But for some people it's still important," she added.

When everything was ready we filtered back into the living room and dined on lentils, kidneys beans, soy chunks with paneer, potatoes with cauliflower, chapattis and rice. Uncle served me black chai tea before adding milk for everyone else and our hostess assured me that nothing except the paneer dish contained dairy and was therefore safe for me to eat. Sadly she was mistaken and shortly after the meal ended I started to feel bloated and unhappy. She emailed us some of the recipes after the tour and the kidney bean dish contained both cream and butter. Sigh.

When we were all full the ladies were invited to try on

saris, but we simply didn't have time. We were meeting Puru for a farewell drink and needed to get back. Thanking our hostess and her family, we headed into the traffic and slowly wound our way back to the other side of New Delhi.

Puru was waiting for us in the designated restaurant and it was here that the official tour ended over drinks, speeches and a pakora or two. Puru had been an excellent tour guide, always patient, always kind and good humoured, very organised and full of information. We couldn't have asked for a better person to take us on our first Indian adventure. I think he only had one day off between our tour ending and the next one beginning, so he had more travelling ahead of him. As for the rest of us, some had flights or trains to catch in the morning which would either take them on further adventures or return them to their families back home. Alan and I didn't have to be at the airport until late in the following evening so we arranged to meet up with Shannon and Beth after breakfast to spend our final day exploring more of Delhi. After bidding a fond farewell to the other lovely people we'd travelled with we made our way back to the hotel for our final night in India, thinking that we couldn't have asked for a nicer, funnier, friendlier bunch to have experienced India with.

A Taxi for Four

The following morning Alan and I met Shannon and Beth at the reception desk and requested a taxi for the day. Shannon was happy to be with us rather than taking a tuk-tuk tour on her own, which she'd done when she first arrived in Delhi. She'd had a similar experience to mine when the driver took her to a store she didn't want to go to and insisted she go in, and she'd had no idea where she was or how to get back to the hotel. I'd been annoyed when it happened to me, but I'd had Alan with me and didn't feel threatened. I could appreciate that it must have been quite scary for Shannon. India is not always the best place for a lady to travel alone.

But today we had the joy of travelling as a foursome with the addition of our taxi driver for the day, Amit. He promised to only take us where we wanted to go with no side excursions to his friends' shops. Beth and Shannon hadn't seen the Parliament Buildings or India Gate, so we went to see those before going anywhere else. The air was less hazy than on our previous visit and there were fewer people milling around, making it much pleasanter than before. I bought a bamboo flute from one of the salesmen who were stalking me, negotiating him down to a hundred rupees and feeling quite pleased with myself. "How much did you pay for that?" asked Amit when we returned to the taxi. I told him and he snorted. "You paid too much." Damn.

Lodi Gardens

After the hustle and bustle of the India Gate we stopped at Lodi Gardens for a bit of tranquillity. This is a popular place for Delhi folk to go for a walk but it was quiet on the day of our visit. The gardens contain various tombs including that of Mohammed Shah, the last of the Sayyid dynasty rulers, which was built in 1444. Another tomb within the gardens is that of Sikander Lodi, built in 1517 and after whom the gardens are named. He was the last Sultan of Delhi from the Lodi dynasty. There were various other tombs in the garden, and to be honest I lost track of who was buried in them. But it was a nice place to wander around, looking at the birds sitting in the trees and watching ducks swim on the murky river.

Khan Market

Our next stop was the Khan Market shopping district, which is popular with both rich Indians and expats in living in central Delhi. Amit told us that Khan Market is the 21st most expensive retail street in the world, which I found very hard to believe.

A central square was surrounded by a variety of shops and restaurants, behind which were two alleyways selling everything from books to household appliances. We passed a "Sensational Sushi" restaurant and a Subway fast food joint. A pet store sold plush dog beds big enough for me to sleep in.

Luxury chocolates were available next to a patisserie and boulangerie. I was intrigued by a store proclaiming itself to be "A-One Exotic Selling Point" and went in to see what passed as "exotic" in Delhi. The owner kindly let me take a picture of his shelves, on which were stacked items such as Marmite, Hellman's mayonnaise, Special K, Pringles and Oreos. It's no wonder expats like to shop at the Khan Market.

Amit suggested that we ate lunch in one of the cafes in the market, directing us to a particularly expensive one. I did a quick survey of what the four of us really wanted to eat, then asked him to take us to a cheap place to have real Indian food. "You want cheap?" he asked in surprise. "Yes." "You want Indian food?" "Yes." He shook his head in apparent bewilderment before dropping us off at The Chimney Café, where we sat at a small table with hard chairs and munched our way through fabulous cheap curries washed down with lime and soda. It was perfect.

Connaught Place

Our final stop of the day was at the Connaught Place shopping district, which Alan and I had tried to see when we first arrived in Delhi. Today the shops were open and people crowded the streets. Amit dropped us off in front of a paint store. "Come back here to find me. And don't get lost. I will look for you." We said we would be back by four as Shannon had a flight to catch, then strolled off to check out the famous CP. The three concentric circles of colonial-style buildings were built by the British in 1933, who used it as their central business area. It's now Delhi's top place for shopping and entertainment.

I could see why our driver told us not to get lost - all the two-story buildings looked the same and some of the big-name stores had numerous locations, making it hard to keep our bearings. It was a strange mix of high-end stores, small craft stores and people sitting on the sidewalk selling hand-made goods. A man sat outside Pepe Jeans of London polishing shoes. Outside The United Colours of Benetton sat a lady selling fabric bags. Near the Marks and Spencers were carts selling Indian snacks, chilled bottled water or ice cream, offering an alternative to the expensive cafes dotted around CP. Worlds collided as modern India intertwined with its past. I spotted a Starbucks and realised this might be my only chance to get a decent coffee in India. "Do you do decaf soy milk cappuccinos?" I asked, not certain what the answer would be. As I settled down in a soft chair to savour my drink I sighed happily. Delhi wasn't all chia tea, bottled water and lime with soda after all.

The hub of CP was filled with market stalls selling just about everything, including sweaters, brand name sports socks, shoes and gym bags. It was packed with people, mostly men, looking for bargains, and they pushed by me if I stopped to look at anything, standing on my toes or elbowing me as they went. I suddenly felt homesick for Canada, where the only pushing that happens is on an ice hockey rink.

And then it was time to go. Shannon, Beth, Alan and I returned to our drop-off point and Amit materialised seemingly out of thin air. He led us to the car and we pulled into the slow-moving traffic. Shannon had a plane to catch and was a bit worried about getting back to the hotel in time. We drove around the CP loop, then drove round it again. On the third time around even our driver was starting to look worried. "The exits are closed and I can't get onto the road I want." We did the loop again and then came to a stop as traffic blocked the road, pointing in every direction. Amit got out of the car and walked away, returning some time later, frowning. "There is a problem, but it's OK. I'll get you back to the hotel."

And off we set, going the wrong way up a one-way street before heading out of CP in the opposite direction to the one we needed. But Amit knew what he was doing, and Shannon arrived back at the hotel with a few minutes to spare before leaping into the taxi waiting to take her to the airport.

Goodbye India!

Alan and I had time for dinner in a restaurant close to the hotel before tossing our backpacks into our final taxi of the trip. “To the airport please.” We smiled at the honking horns and laughed when a tuk-tuk going the wrong way around a roundabout puttered past us.

When we first arrived in India I'd expected it to be quite an adventure, and I'd been right. It had been different from my expectations, but mostly in a good way. I'd anticipated mad drivers, crowded streets, dirt, dust and beggars, but I hadn't been expecting to be hounded by young men with cameras at every step. I thought I would see ruins and shacks but hadn't realised I would visit enormous fortresses, huge palaces and ornately carved temples. I saw more cows than I thought I would and encountered fewer camels. The vast numbers of stray dogs made me happier about my choice to have rabies shots before the trip. I'd eaten curry for breakfast, lunch, dinner and snacks, and apart from problems arising from hidden dairy ingredients I hadn't suffered any ill effects. I'd planned for stomach upsets but caught the 'flu instead. I'd had more cold showers than hot, waded through flooded bathrooms and slept on the hardest beds I've ever encountered. I'm glad I went. But would I go back?

If you'd asked me that question as I sat on the plane leaving Delhi my answer would have been a resounding "Oh hell no!" But with the passage of time I feel differently. Linus and Lucinda recently stayed with us in Canada and told us of their trip to Goa. It sounded… interesting. So will I go back to India? Yes, I think I might… but I'm not sure how I'm going to break the news to Alan. Perhaps I'll wait until we're flying back from our upcoming return trip to Japan. Two weeks, two backpacks and two Japan Rail passes to get us from Osaka to Kumamoto and back. We'll be staying in Air BnB apartments, riding the trains, eating noodles and drinking sake. There'll be castles and shrines and, if we're really lucky, cherry blossoms. We're hoping to meet a traditional sword smith. Now that sounds like fun! And, unlike our time in India, we'll do it all without being constantly stalked by young men with cameras.

Travel Books by the same author:

Tall Travel Tales: Japan
Tokyo, Takayama and Beyond.
ISBN: 978-0-9920826-4-2 (Paperback)
ISBN: 978-0-9920826-5-9 (E-Book)

Tall Travel Tales: India
Delhi, Agra, Rajasthan and Rats.
ISBN: 978-0-9920826-6-6 (Paperback)
ISBN: 978-0-9920826-7-3 (E-Book)

Tall Travel Tales: Japan
Osaka, Takamatsu, Kumamoto and more.
(Expected release date December 2016)
ISBN: 978-0-9920826-8-0 (Paperback)
ISBN: 978-0-9920826-9-7 (E-Book)

Cookbooks by the same author:

HELP! There's a VEGAN Coming for Dinner!
ISBN: 978-0-9920826-0-4 (Paperback)
ISBN: 978-0-9920826-1-1 (E-Book)

HELP! There's a VEGAN Coming for Dinner - Japanese Style
ISBN: 978-0-9920826-2-8 (Paperback)
ISBN: 978-0-9949097-0-1 (E-Book)

HELP! There's a VEGAN Coming for Dinner - Indian Style
ISBN: 978-0-9920826-3-5 (Paperback)
ISBN: 978-0-9949097-1-8 (E-Book)

Check out more titles at

Art and Soul Interiors Publishing

http://artandsoulinteriors.com

Lightning Source UK Ltd.
Milton Keynes UK
UKOW07f1527221216
290661UK00010B/52/P

9 780992 082666